Sharing Lives

Bert de Ruiter

Sharing Lives

Overcoming Our Fear of Islam

Bibliographic information published by the Deutsche Nationalbibliothek
The Deutsche Nationalbibliothek lists this publication in the Deutsche Nationalbibliografie; detailed bibliographic data are available in the Internet at http://dnb.d-nb.de.

ISBN 978-3-902669-10-0
OM Books
Passaustr. 19, 4030 Linz, Austria

ISBN 978-3-941750-22-7
VTR Publications
Gogolstr. 33, 90475 Nürnberg, Germany, http://www.vtr-online.eu

This publication is based on a dissertation for the degree of DMin in Christian-Muslim Relation at Bakke Graduate University, Seattle, USA.

Cover Design: Simon Specht, OM EAST (Austria)
Type and Layout by Heike Scharmann, Wetzlar (Germany)
Printed in the UK by Lightning Source.

Contents

Chapter Two
Dealing with Fear of Islam

Chapter Three
Helping Christians to Overcome their Islamophobia

Chapter Four
Sharing Lives: A Course for Christians

Chapter Five
Testing and Evaluating Course Sharing Lives

Chapter Six
Summary, Conclusions and Recommendations

List of Tables

Acknowledgments

A project of this nature cannot be done in isolation. Many people have shared in this venture, and I would like to acknowledge their contributions. I want to thank Robert Calvert for recommending me to Bakke Graduate University and suggesting that I start the D. Min. program. This program has changed my life and has helped me to become a more thoughtful practitioner. I want to thank Dr. Ida Glaser for being my dissertation supervisor and for her rigorous critique that has helped to make this document as good as possible, as well as the members of my Personal Learning Community: Christiaan Kwantes, Siebren Woudstra, Wim Reinders, Ben Wentsel, Niekie Waaning, Andreas Maurer, Elsie Maxwell, and David Greenlee for their prayers, encouragement, and feedback. In addition, I want to thank Dr. John and Mrs. Pansy Culpepper for editing this document and Bakke Graduate University for giving me a scholarship, which enabled me to take part in the D. Min. program. Special thanks are extended to my organization Operation Mobilization for allowing me to take time off to devote to this study program.

Finally, and most importantly, I want to thank my wife Jenny, my son Jefta, my daughter-in-law Jessica, and my daughter Tamar for putting up with the many hours that I was not available for them because of my studies.

Last, but not least, I want to thank my heavenly Father, for granting me the privilege to serve him among Muslims and for enabling me to learn more from him and grow closer to him in understanding his passion for Muslims in Europe.

Abstract

This dissertation argues that the single greatest hindrance to Christian witness amongst Muslims in Europe is fear. A short course was developed in order to help Christians overcome their fear of Islam and Muslims and to encourage Christians to share their lives with Muslims and the truth of the Gospel with the purpose of attracting them to Christ.

Many European Christians share a widespread fear of Islam, termed *Islamophobia*. They fear that Europe will gradually turn into *Eurabia*, or Islamic domination of Europe, and they ignore the efforts of Muslims to adapt to the European context, while not necessarily giving up their faith developments, a situation pointing to a future scenario of *Euro-Islam*, or Islam being Europeanized.

When one looks at fear theologically, that fear is rooted in the fallen condition of man and involves a tendency to exclude anybody that threatens one's identity. On the other side, the more thoughts, attitude, and behavior are guided by God's self-giving love manifested at the cross of Golgotha, the more one will be able to respond in grace towards Muslims. While this change of attitude from fear to grace is a key requirement for Christians to share their lives with Muslims, many books and courses that have been developed to help Christians relate to Muslims do not explicitly deal with this but concentrate on providing information about Islam and skills to help share the Gospel with Muslims.

Consequently, a new course entitled Sharing Lives has been developed. The testing of this course has shown it results in a changed attitude towards Islam and Muslims and a commitment to establishing contact with Muslims. With some further changes to diminish the course's weaknesses and make better use of its strengths, this course could become an instrument in God's hand to encourage Christians in Europe to share their lives with Muslims.

Introduction

The Problem

For the past thirteen years, my ministry focused on encouraging Christians and churches throughout Europe to reach out to their Muslim neighbors with the truth and love of God. I was responsible for overseeing Christian ministries among Muslims in several European countries (France, UK, the Netherlands, Belgium and Spain). I also helped establish new ministries (Italy, Germany, Austria, and Switzerland). In addition, I encouraged Christian workers among Muslims in the Balkans and taught at conferences and in churches across Europe.

It is encouraging to see that during these years more churches and Christians have developed a heart for their Muslim neighbors. It is also encouraging to learn of Muslims in Europe who have come to accept the Lord Jesus Christ as their Lord and Savior and have become active members of European churches or have been instrumental to establish migrant churches.

Despite this, I have seen that Muslims are more willing to hear about the Gospel than Christians are willing to share the Gospel with Muslims. I have spoken in churches in cities across Europe that meet in predominantly Muslim neighborhoods while the members of these same churches do not establish any meaningful relationships with the Muslims living around them.

Throughout Europe I found Christian communities and Muslim communities living in close proximity to each other, individuals passing each other in the streets, standing next to each other waiting for the bus, or sharing apartment buildings, classrooms and business canteens, but essentially strangers to each other.

I asked myself: what is it that hinders Christians from sharing their lives with Muslims? People don't have to fly across the world to meet Muslims, but just have to cross the street, but what keeps them from doing so? Is it lack of information? It does not seem like it. There are plenty of good books on Islam, and I have taught in many schools, churches and living rooms across Europe and provided those present with as accurate information about Islam as I could. But it didn't seem to result in more friendships between Christian and Muslims.

Meanwhile, Islam is "hot" in today's media. Many Christians talk about the Muslims who burn churches in Indonesia, persecute Christians in Egypt, fly airplanes into buildings, and hijack people in Yemen. For a long time these events occurred far away. But then trains where bombed by Muslims in Madrid and in the London underground, and a Dutch television producer was killed by a Moroccan in Amsterdam. Also it is observed that many Muslims seem reluctant to adapt to "Christian" European rights, claiming their own rights instead.

The hypothesis underlying this dissertation is that the average European Christian is afraid of Muslims, and that fear is the single biggest factor preventing them from relating to Muslims. This fear often means that even Christians, who agree that it is necessary to share the Gospel with Muslims, see sharing the Gospel as separate from sharing one's life. Preliminary investigations in reading about Islam in Europe, the study of *Islamophobia* and personal research among groups of Christians in the Netherlands appears to support this hypothesis.[1] Therefore the problem addressed in this dissertation is: How can Christians in Europe overcome their negative attitude of fear for Islam and Muslims and learn to respond with grace and share their lives with Muslims? This dissertation describes a tool that could make a useful contribution to solving this problem, namely a five session training course called Sharing Lives.

[1] A questionnaire I conducted among forty seven Christians in the Netherlands showed that despite the condemnation of a negative attitude towards Muslims by the majority of the respondents, the main attitude that surfaced when looking at the outcome of the questionnaire is a negative one, namely: suspicion leaning towards fear. This fear, based upon and fed by prejudices, is strongest among the African respondents. For more information, see chapter 5 and Appendix E.

The Outcome

The expected outcome of the research represented by this dissertation is to describe a rationale and a process whereby Muslims in Europe will have Christian friends. One of the ways to accomplish this is to provide a tool that could help Christians in Europe to overcome their fear of Islam and Muslims and become friends of Muslims and present the truth of the Gospel to them, thereby giving them the opportunity to know Christ.

The Scope

In light of my particular ministry, which is Europe-wide geographically, the scope of this dissertation project is the continent of Europe, with a particular emphasis on Western Europe. Having such a wide scope means one cannot apply everything that is said in this paper to each and every country and city in Europe. The question of attitudes towards Muslims by Christians in Europe is huge and complex. Differences in attitude, clear as well as subtle, will inevitably vary widely dependent upon different contexts but this document will argue that fear is the single greatest hindrance to Christian witness amongst Muslims in Europe, irrespective of country and denomination.

The Context

Demographic Statistics

According to the Zentral-Institut Islam-Archiv-Deutschland, there are 53.7 million Muslims[2] in Europe, with 15.9 million residing in the European Union. Out of a European population of ap-

[2] One should not forget that among them are both fundamentalists and liberals, both cultural and conservative Muslims.

proximately 680 million Europeans, according to the institute 7.9 percent are Muslim.[3]

Data obtained from the World Christian Database indicates that in 2005 the number of Christians in Europe, including Russia, was 531 million. This number includes Christians of Protestant, Orthodox, Roman Catholic, and other faiths, many of whom are counted as Christians only on the baptismal rolls of their churches. In their European Spiritual Estimate (2005), the European Missions Research Group (emRG) estimates that 72.7 percent of Europeans are culturally affiliated with Christianity.[4] When it comes to defining Europeans who are not only culturally, but practically followers of Jesus Christ, the terms used and the numbers given become confusing.

The European Believers Report (2007) estimates that 1.1 percent or about eight million) of Europeans are *believers*.[5] Author Philip Jenkins estimates that the number of *committed believing Christians* in *Western* Europe is between sixty and seventy million.[6]

[3] The *Zentral-Institut Islam-Archiv-Deutschland,* founded in 1927 is the oldest Islamic institution in the German speaking world. They obtained the information on Muslims in Europe from European embassies and agencies for statistics in European countries. In these statistics Europe includes Russia and the western (European part) of Turkey. The information was received from Mr. Gerhard Isa Moldenhauer of this centre through an e-mail received on May 13, 2007. For more details (in German) see Appendix A.

[4] Scott Friderich, "The European Spiritual Estimate," *Emrg Home Page*, 2005, http://www.emrg.dzubinski.com/ (accessed April 14, 2009). The European Spiritual Estimate (ESE) is a survey administered by the European Missions Research Group (emRG) from August 1 to December 12, 2005. The general purpose of the survey is to provide a reasonable estimate of the level of Christian commitment in Europe.

[5] Ruth Robinson, "Ebr 2007 (revised)," *Emrgnet*, 2007, http://www.emrgnet.eu/wordpress/data/europe-level/ebr-2007/ (accessed April 14, 2009). In this report 'a believer' is defined as one who has chosen a personal, obedient relationship with Jesus, the only way to God and to eternal life in heaven). According to the report these people part of the "harvest force" in God's Kingdom work.

[6] Philip Jenkins, *God's Continent: Christianity, Islam and Europe's Religious Crisis* (Oxford: Oxford University Press, 2007), 56. He defines these as Christians who assert that religion plays a very important part in their lives and who attend church regularly.

Operation World counts 17.2 million *Evangelicals,* 13.8 million *charismatics,* 4.3 million *Pentecostals* in Europe.[7] David Barrett in the World Christian Database, 2001 reckons there to be 17.9 million *Evangelicals* and 24.9 million *charismatic* and *Pentecostal* believers in Europe.[8]

The European Missions Research Group (emRG) estimates that about 4.12 percent of Europe's population or about thirty million are what they call *Gospel Oriented Christians,* who follow Jesus Christ and are concerned about the spiritual condition of their fellow man.[9] When the word 'Christian' is used in this dissertation, reference is being made to committed, Gospel oriented, evangeli-

[7] Patrick Johnstone and Jason Mandryk, *Operation World* (Carlisle: Paternoster Lifestyle, 2001), 52. Operation World is a prayer handbook and reference guide, with informative fuel for prayer about every country of the world.

Evangelicals are defined as: "1 All affiliated Christians of denominations that are evangelical in theology which means emphasizing a) the Lord Jesus Christ as the sole source of salvation through faith in Him; b) personal faith and conversion with regeneration by the Holy Spirit; c) a recognition of the inspired Word of God as the only basis for faith and Christian living; d) commitment to biblical witness, evangelism and mission that brings others to faith in Christ. 2 The proportion of the affiliated Christians in other denominations (that are not wholly evangelical in theology) who would hold evangelical views. 3 The proportion of affiliated Christians in denominations in non-Western nations (where doctrinal positions are less well defined) that would be regarded as Evangelicals by those in the above categories." Johnstone and Mandryk, 756.

Charismatics are defined as: "Those who testify to a renewing experience of the Holy Spirit and present exercise of the gifts of the Spirit such as *glossalalia,* healing, prophecy and miracles. The Charismatic renewal or 'Second Wave' Pentecostalism has generally remained within mainline denominations. There is a further 'Third Wave' renewal movement with many characteristics of the Second Wave but with less open identification with Pentecostalism or the Charismatic Movement. Second and Third Wave Charismatics are counted as a single entity in this book." Johnstone en Mandryk, 755.

Pentecostals are defined as: "Those affiliated to specifically Pentecostal denominations committed to a Pentecostal theology usually including a post-conversion experience of a baptism in the Spirit, present exercise of the gifts of the Spirit and speaking in tongues." Johnstone en Mandryk, 757.

[8] David Barrett, ed., *World Christian Encyclopedia* (Oxford: Oxford University Press, 2001).

[9] Scott Friderich, "The European Spiritual Estimate", emRG Home Page, http://www.emrg.dzubinski.com (accessed April 14, 2009).

cal, charismatic, and Pentecostal believers, whose numbers roughly resemble the number of Muslims in Europe.

The Biblical and Theological Basis

Fear of the Lord Casts out Fear of Men

Fear is a natural basic element and instinct of human nature. Some fear is positive, as the self-protective instinct that gives warning of danger. On the other hand, fear can also be negative and a hindrance for Christians to become all God wants them to be and do. All fear is based on perception. Several times in the Bible fear is the result of seeing God in the shadow of the circumstances, instead of seeing the circumstances in the shadow of God.[10]

This document presupposes that one needs to fear God more than men. Throughout the Bible there is a close link between the fear of the Lord and the fear of men. "Fear of the Lord" is a term that summarizes the desired attitude of man towards God and is a paradoxical term, which includes trust in his love, respect for his holiness and fear for his anger. "Fear of the Lord" expresses a state of intimacy and distance at the same time as well as majesty and humanity, consuming fire, and trustful relationship. God wants mankind to fear him more than anything and anybody else (Ps. 76:7; Luke 12:5; Is. 8: 11, 12, 13) and the more one fears the Lord the less we are afraid of men (Ps. 112: 1, 7, 8; Proverbs 14:26; 19:23). It can also be the other way round: One can fear people more, because one doesn't fear God enough (Is. 57:11)

Proverbs 29:25 states "Fear of man will prove to be a snare, but whoever trusts in the LORD is kept safe." In this verse the panic induced by human threat is compared to trust in the Lord. A snare represents being caught in a fatal situation. The panic-stricken person does not react reasonably and if he or she does, he or she may do the wrong thing.

[10] See Joshua 14:8; 1 Samuel 13:7; 14:6; 17:24, 26,32; 2 Kings 25:26; Jeremiah 42:11; Nehemiah 4:10,14; Matthew 14:28,29, 30

Fear entered the world after humanity's relationship with God was broken as a result of sin. Adam and Eve, the first humans, became afraid of God (Genesis 3:10). In the last book of the Bible, it is revealed that fear will not be part of God's eternal Kingdom (Revelation 21: 3, 4). In this document I want to consider the fear of Islam and Muslims, in the light of the fear of the Lord.

The Living God is a Missionary God

From the beginning of human history when God called out to Adam: "Where are you?" (Gen. 3:9) God has been searching for those that have broken fellowship with him. In the context of this document this calling means that God also calls Muslims in order to bring them under the Lordship of Jesus Christ.

God's Instrument to Reach the World is His Church

The most important means God uses to carry out his plan on earth is his church (Eph. 3:10), which is the body of Christ (Eph. 1:23). God has chosen the Church with Christ at the very center of his plan to reconcile the world to himself. (Eph. 1:20–23).

Muslims Can Only Be Saved Through Jesus Christ

There are three main positions that Christians hold with reference to how they view other religions, which are pluralism, inclusivism, and exclusivism. This dissertation presupposes the third view or exclusivism. According to this view only those who place their faith in the Christ of the Bible are saved.

Integration of Proclamation and Incarnation is Needed

The Gospel is holistic. The church is not just to proclaim the Gospel of the Kingdom (Matt 24:14), but also to display the life of the Kingdom (Matthew 5–7) and to perform the works of the Kingdom. The "Word became flesh" (John 1:14) referring to the incarnation of Jesus is the model par excellence for the ministry of Christians in this world.

This model was also one of the Apostle Paul's ways of witnessing about Jesus Christ. He writes about this in his letter to the church in Thessalonica: "We loved you so much that we were delighted to share with you not only the gospel but our lives as well, because you had become so dear to us." (1 Thess. 2:8)

Paul's Epistle to the Thessalonians was his earliest epistle written during his second missionary journey around AD 52. Paul and Silas had preached the gospel in Thessalonica less than a year previously. They had to leave Thessalonica before they completed their work due to the great opposition to the Gospel by the Jews. While in Athens Timothy brought Paul word from the church in Thessalonica (1 Thess.3:6), together with some questions that they had raised. Paul wrote his first epistle in response to their overture.

In chapter one Paul begins with a greeting followed by thanksgiving for the work of God and the response of the Thessalonians to the Gospel. In chapter two Paul gives a review of his ministry to the Thessalonians (2:1–12). In light of the slander Paul had received from the religious Judaizers who claimed he was only out for personal gain, Paul reviews his and his team's ministry and emphasizes their motives and conduct. Paul refers to his own character and manner of living for proof of what he was saying to the Thessalonians.

He emphasizes his and his coworkers' boldness in proclaiming the Gospel in the face of opposition (1–2), the purity of their motives and actions (3–6), their friendly and loving attitude (7–8), and their holy, righteous, and blameless behavior (10–12). For the purpose of this dissertation, two things from this passage are relevant: (1) proclamation needs to go together with demonstration; and (2) sharing the Gospel needs to go together with sharing one's life.

Nine times in this letter Paul writes "You know" referring to the Thessalonians firsthand knowledge of Paul's life. Paul's emphasis on motives and conduct in the midst of proclaiming the gospel makes clear that the manner in which one proclaims the gospel and the character of the messengers needs to be in harmony with the content of the gospel. In his commentary on 1 Thessalonians, Theologian J. Vernon McGee believes that Paul's exemplified in Thessalonica that the greatest sermon one will ever preach is by the life that one lives:

> If you were asked to choose, what would you select as the greatest sermon of the apostle Paul . . .? I would choose his life in Thessalonica. His greatest sermon was not in writing or speaking, but in walking. It was not in exposition, but in experience; not in his profession, but in his practice. He took his text from James 2:26, faith without works is dead and he made his points on the pavement of the streets of Thessalonica.[11]

In verse eight the Apostle Paul points out that he and his team had a genuine love for the people they shared the Gospel with. They not only delivered a message, but also gave themselves. In his commentary on this verse, scholar F. F. Bruce writes that "to share their own lives involved utter self-denial, spending and being spent in the interest of others." He also points out that the word used for *life* here is *Psuche,* which is the seat of affection and will and concludes that "the meaning is not simply we were willing to give (lay down) our lives for you but we were willing to give ourselves to you, to put ourselves at your disposal, without reservation."[12]

In his commentary, Ernest Best applies Paul's example to all missionaries when he writes that "the true missionary is not someone specialized in the delivery of the message but someone who's whole being, completely committed to a message which demands all, is communicated to his hearers."[13]

[11] J. Vernon McGee, *1 & 2 Thessalonians (Through the Bible commentary series)* (Nashville, Tenessee: Thomas Nelson, Inc, 1995), 35ff; quoted in *http://www.preceptaustin.org/1thessalonians_21-htm* (accessed: January 24, 2009).

[12] F. F. Bruce, *1 and 2 Thessalonians*, ed. Bruce M. Metzger, *Word Biblical Commentary* (Dallas: Word Incorporated, 1982), 23ff.

[13] Ernest Best, *Black's New Testament Commentaries*, ed., *A commentary of the First and Second Epistles to the Thessalonians* (Peabody, Massachusetts: Hendrickson Publishers, 1993), 102,103.

Applying the truth of this verse to evangelism among Muslims, three things stand out: (1) Evangelism is a lifestyle, not just an activity. Verbal sharing of the Gospel needs to be integrated in one's life and linked with addressing social needs that are a result of a broken relationship with the Lord; (2) In order for Muslims to have an accurate understanding of Jesus Christ and the biblical faith, they need to see an expression of it in the lives of people they know and trust;[14] (3) Christians who want to incarnate the truth of the Gospel to Muslims need to have an accurate understanding of Muslims in the context of a relationship of love and trust. Loving and understanding the people who need the Gospel is vital for sharing the Gospel with them. All three aspects mean that there needs to be close proximity between Christians and Muslims, or to put it differently, Christians need to share their lives with Muslims.

Background and Description of the Outline

The desired outcome of this dissertation is that Christians in Europe share their lives with Muslims. One's willingness to do so is related to how one perceives the intentions of the Muslim community in Europe. It is important to understand that one's attitude to Islam colors one's perception of the future of Islam in Europe. Chapter 1 looks at two possible future scenarios, namely *Eurabia*, which expects that Europe will be Islamized and *Euro-Islam*, which expects that Islam will be Europeanized, and determine which one is the most likely to take place and why.

After having seen that the majority of Muslims in Europe seeks to live out their faith in harmony with European values, one won-

[14] J. Dudley Woodberry, G. Shubin, and G. Marks, "Why Muslims Follow Jesus," *Christianity Today*, October 24, 2007. Dr. Woodberry, professor of Islamic Studies at Fuller, researched what attracts Muslims to follow Jesus. Between 1991 and 2007 about 750 Muslims who have decided to follow Christ filled out an extensive questionnaire. The number one reason respondents—from 30 countries and 50 ethnic groups—representing every major region of the Muslim world, listed, for their decision to follow Christ was the lifestyle of the Christians among them.

ders why it is not more obvious to the average European, including Christians. Could it be that the negative lenses of most Europeans prevent them from seeing positive developments?

Looking at this question in more detail in chapter 2, one discovers that many Christians, instead of being agents of social change, reflect the *Islamophobia* of the wider European society. I will analyze the underlying causes and suggest ways to overcome such an attitude and develop another way, namely one of grace.

If such an attitude change is so important in order for Christians to share their lives with Muslims, it is important to learn how books and courses that are designed to encourage Christians to relate to Muslims deal with this. Therefore, chapter 3 analyzes nine books and seven courses, and particularly looks at whether these materials deal with the issue of eliminating or decreasing fear or even heighten the level of fear for Islam and Muslims through their tone and style. It will be pointed out that most of the researched books and courses do not sufficiently address the importance of a change of attitude from fear to grace towards Muslims and conclude that a new course is needed.

Chapter 4 describes the background, objectives, and content of such a course entitled Sharing Lives that is developed as a tool to help Christians to overcome their fear of Islam and Muslims, be willing to become a friend of Muslims, and incarnate the truth of the Gospel to them, thereby attracting them to Christ.

In order to find out whether Sharing Lives accomplishes its objectives, this course has been run as a pilot during the months of November and December 2008 in three groups in the Netherlands. Chapter 5 evaluates these pilots, analyzes the outcomes, and the responses of the participants. Chapter 6 summarizes the findings in the previous chapters and draws out some conclusions and recommendations for the future.

Chapter One
The Future of Islam in Europe

Introduction

One's attitude to Islam colors one's perception of the future of Islam in Europe and one's perception of the future of Islam in Europe influences one's attitude to Islam and Muslims. In this chapter I will look at two scenarios concerning the future of Islam in Europe, which are in opposition to each other. *Eurabia* is a term coined by the British-Swiss Jewish historian Bat Ye'or and describes the expectation that Europe will be Islamized.[1] In contrast *Euro-Islam* is a concept introduced by Bassam Tibi, a Syrian born Muslim and German citizen, which sees Islam becoming Europeanized.[2]

An attitude of fear of Islam and Muslims is often caused by or gives support to the expectation of Europe becoming *Eurabia*. Not only among Europeans in general, but particularly among Christians in Europe, the *Eurabia* scenario seems to receive more support popular than the *Euro-Islam* scenario. For example, a questionnaire carried out by me among several groups of Christians in the Netherlands, shows that 60 percent of the respondents agree with Geert Wilders, a Dutch MP and head of an extreme right party, who warns against the growing Islamization of the Netherlands and Europe.[3] In September 2008, I received an e-mail from a Dutch Christian citing examples of how Europe submits to the demands of Muslims.[4]

[1] Bat Ye'or, *Eurabia: the Euro-Arab axis* (Madison, NJ: Fairleigh Dickinson University Press, 2005)

[2] Bassam Tibi, "Europeanisation, Not Islamisation," *Sign And Sight.com*, http://signandsight.com/features/1258.html. (accessed April 14, 2009).

[3] For further information see chapter 5 and Appendix D.

[4] Hans Holtrop in an e-mail,entitled "Europa is bezig zich in een hoog tempo te onderwerpen aan de Islam" (Europe is Islamizing in a rapid speed) on September 9, 2008

Those who expect the *Eurabia* scenario consider Islam to be a problem in Europe. They speak of a clash of civilizations pointing out that Islam threatens European values of secularization and freedom of speech. They refer to extreme Muslims who reject European values and who seek to establish a *Khalifat* in Europe in which the shari'a law becomes the constitution. People with an attitude of *Islamophobia* often agree with or only see indications that support a *Eurabia* scenario, but they seem unable or unwilling to see the developments that support a *Euro-Islam* scenario.

Those who expect the *Euro-Islam* scenario point to Islam's adaptation to Europe as seen in the emergence of Islamic political and civic leaders and associations. They point, as well, to changes in religious authority, changes in describing Islam's status as a minority culture, a desire for gender equality, and changes in interpreting the meaning of *shari'a*.

In this chapter it will be argued that the majority of Muslims are willing to find their place in Europe. Therefore a *Euro-Islam* scenario is more likely than a *Eurabian* scenario. Nevertheless there often is reluctance on the part of European governments and citizens, including Christians, to create space for Islam and Muslims resulting in an attitude of cold tolerance.

Background on Islam in Europe

Islam has increasingly become part of Europe's social, cultural and political and religious landscape. In the course of a few decades, it has become Europe's second religion after Christianity. The arrival of millions of Muslims in Europe from the 1960s has permanently changed the future of Europe and has been called

which was sent to all Christian organizations and institutions in the Netherlands in September 2008. Holtrop, a Dutch Christian, cites many examples from newspaper articles in France, the Netherlands and Belgium of how Europe is submitting to Islam.

"the greatest religio-demographic change on the European continent since the time of the Reformation"[5]

Since the 1950s Western Europe has seen the arrival of migrant workers and asylum-seekers, many of whom come from Muslim countries. For the first ten years the only arrivals were men of working age, whose main aim was to earn money to send back home and then to return home. This expectation never materialized largely due to changes in immigration laws. They decided to stay in Europe and their families came to join them. This radically altered the structure of the Muslim community in Western Europe leading to new social and religious priorities and demands on the host community.

In the Eastern part of Europe, the emergence of the Balkan Muslim population as an autonomous political actor is one of the major changes of the last decade. The Islamic religious institutions of the Balkans experienced a renewal of activity, creating their own political parties, newspapers, cultural associations and charitable societies or intellectual forums.[6] European Muslims come primarily from countries formerly colonized or dominated by the most influential European countries.[7]

Robert J. Pauly identifies the following key characteristics of Islam in Europe:

1. Geographically, most Muslims are located in low-rent housing in the suburbs on the peripheries of major urban centers in Europe.

[5] Penelope Johnstone and Jan Slomp, "Islam and the churches in Europe: A Christian perspective," *Journal of Muslim Minority Affairs*, 18., 2 (October 1998), 355.

[6] Ibrahimi Nexhat, "Islam's First Contacts With The Balkan Nations," *Yahoo! Geocities*, http://www.geocities.com/Athens/Delphi/6875/nexhat.html. (accessed April 14, 2009).

[7] Jocelyne Cesari calls them "a postcolonial minority culture". Jocelyne Cesari, *When Islam and Democracy Meet: Muslims in Europe and the United States* (New York: Palgrave, 2004), 12.

2. Demographically, Muslim communities in Europe are younger and possess higher growth rates than is true of the European majority.
3. Economically, Muslims face considerably worse economic circumstances than the majority of others living in Europe (e. g. high unemployment, resulting in perpetual struggle for subsistence, housing problems).
4. Socially, the Muslim community in Europe is quite diverse when we look at their ethnic and cultural background and their religious denomination and practice.[8]

Future Scenarios

When speaking of the future of Islam in Europe, two opposing scenarios dominate the media presentation, namely that of *Eurabia* and *Euro-Islam.* In the remainder of this chapter I will look at several religious, social, and political aspects of Muslims in Europe in order to get some clarity on which of the two scenarios is most likely to take place, or whether both miss the mark.

Eurabia

Introduction

This scenario expects that Europe will be Islamized. The term was originally coined by the British-Swiss Jewish historian Bat Ye'or in 2005 in her book *Eurabia: the Euro-Arab axis* to describe what she identified as a secret project between European politicians and the Arab world for the "Islamization" of Europe.[9]

[8] Robert J. Pauly, *Islam in Europe: Integration or Marginalization* (Aldershot, UK: Ashgate, 2004). Although Pauly focuses particularly on France, Germany, and the UK, his conclusions generally apply to most European countries.

[9] Bat Ye'or, *Eurabia: the Euro-Arab axis* (Madison, NJ: Fairleigh Dickinson University Press, 2005). The term *Eurabia* is unfortunate since not all Muslims in Europe are Arabs.

Those who see this scenario as true, such as the Italian journalist Oriana Fallaci, historian Bernard Lewis, author Robert Spencer, and Dutch MP Geert Wilders, generally believe that Islam is hostile to and incompatible with the values of the western world. In the view of these advocates the presence of a substantial numbers of Muslims in Europe is a deliberate strategy which will produce the result that Muslims will form a demographic majority within a few generations, that all or most Muslims seek to Islamize Europe, and that part of the European political and cultural elite supports this goal.

According to the worst-case *Eurabian* predictions, by the end of the twenty-first century, most of Europe's cities will be overrun by Arabic-speaking foreign immigrants, much of the continent will be living under Islamic *shari'a* law, and Christianity will have ceased to exist or be reduced to a state of *dhimmitude*[10]. In the *Eurabia* scenario Christians and Jews will become oppressed minorities in a sea of Islam; churches and cathedrals will be replaced by mosques and minarets; the call to prayer will echo from Paris to Rotterdam and to London; and the remnants of "Judeo-Christian" Europe will have been reduced to small enclaves in a world of bearded Arabic-speakers and *burka*-clad women.[11]

Those who expect the *Eurabian* scenario consider Islam a problem to modernization in Europe. They particularly speak of a clash of civilizations and describe how Islam threatens European values such as secularization and freedom of speech. Also the presence of extreme Islamists in Europe is used to support a *Eurabian* scenario. I will look at this scenario in more detail below.

[10] *Dhimmitude* is derived from the *dhimmi,* which literally means "protected". The term *Dhimmitude* has several meanings, denoting "an attitude of concession, surrender and appeasement towards Islamic demands".

[11] For a critical analysis, see Carr Matt, "You are Now Entering Eurabia," *Race & class* 48, no. 1 (2006): 1–22.

Islam as a Perceived Problem

European societies respond predominantly negatively to the growing visibility of Islam in their midst. Dr. Jocelyne Cesari, Research Associate at the Centre for Middle Eastern Studies and visiting professor at Harvard University, who has done extensive research on Islam as a minority in secular and democratic contexts, believes that in Europe we can speak of "a meta-narrative on Islam" that portrays Islam "as a problem or an obstacle to modernization."[12]

A Clash of Civilizations?

The advocates of *Eurabia* believe that the tensions in many European societies created by the arrival of millions of Muslims, is a result of a clash of civilizations.[13] Others say it is a result of ethnic and religious Muslim-Christian tensions in the West.[14] Also many Christians consider Islam a threat to European civilization. A questionnaire that I conducted shows that 46 percent of the Christians agree with and another 33 percent did not explicitly disagree with the statement "Islam is a threat to our civilization."[15]

Those who define the tense relationship between Islam and Europe as a clash of civilizations point out that there are differenc-

[12] Cesari, *Islam and Democracy*, 21.

[13] Samuel Huntington's influential book *The Clash of Civilizations and the Remaking of World Order*, presents a model of explaining future interactions among states in the international system. In this book Huntington considers the Islamic resurgence one of the main challenges of Western civilization. Samuel P. Huntington, *The Clash of Civilizations and the Remaking of World Order* (London: Simon & Schuster, 1997).

[14] Robert J. Pauly, *Islam in Europe: Integration or Marginalization?*, 21. Pauly believes Huntington misperceives the nature of the threat Islam poses to the West. "Put simply, Huntington issues a warning as to the potential for instability rooted in a clash between the Western and Islamic civilizations that is actually more likely to develop as a product of rising ethnic and religious Muslim-Christian tensions in the West."

[15] For more details, see chapter 5 and appendix D.

es between cultures of Western and Islamic societies.[16] Some, like Huntington believe such differences rest on political systems, for example democracy and its varied forms.[17] Others consider social values, including gender equality and sexual liberalization and specifically identified as homosexuality, abortion, and divorce, the main clash between the West and Islam.[18] Those who fear or expect a *Eurabia*, particularly refer to two values that people hold dear in Europe and which seem to be under threat due to the presence of Muslims in Europe, namely secularism and freedom of expression.

Islam: A Threat to Secularization?

The arrival of a large number of Muslims in Europe has reopened the file on the relationship between the church and the state in Europe.[19] Secularization is a fundamental aspect of democracy in Europe. In Europe the term secularization has an ideological function and manifests itself as an element of European identity.[20]

[16] It is hard to speak of a single Islamic civilization or culture, because there are substantial contrasts among one billion people living in diverse Islamic nations.

[17] Huntington considers the separation of spiritual and temporal authority, the concept of the centrality of law, social pluralism, representative bodies and individualism part of the core of Western civilization, which are significantly different from other cultures, causing a clash of civilization. Huntington, 56–78.

[18] Pipa Norris and Roger Inglehart, researched the political and social values in many countries around the world and concluded that the most basic cultural fault line between the West and Islam concern issues of gender equality and sexual liberation. See Pipa Norris and Roger Inglehart, "Religion and Politics in the Islamic World," in *Sacred and Secular: Religion and Politics,* 133–156.

[19] According to Fetzer en Soper "the migration and settlement of large numbers of Muslims into Western Europe poses a new challenge to the existing church-state arrangements in countries and has resurrected somewhat dormant religious disputes." Joel Fetzer and Chris Soper, *Muslims and the State in Britain, France and Germany* (Cambridge: Cambridge University Press, 2005), 6.

[20] Wikipedia, "Secularization", Wikipedia, http://en.wikipedia.org/wiki/Secularization (accessed April 13, 2009). According to Wikipedia, secularization generally refers to the process of transformation by which a society migrates from close identification with religious institutions to a more separated relationship.

One characteristic of the secularist mindset is the idea that religion has no share in the common good of societies. This attitude is practically unanimous in Western Europe, no matter what the relationship is between the state and organized religion. It also includes both religious organizations' independence from most forms of political authority and the protection of religious freedom guaranteed by that same power. Secularization also leads to the tendency to discount or ignore matters of religion in social interactions between citizens and stands for the diminished social influence of religion and its institutions in public life.

Those who expect a *Eurabia* scenario point out that the secularization of Europe makes the various manifestations of Islam in Europe problematic or even unacceptable. Islam is considered to be the diametrical opposite of the principle of secularization. The establishment of Islam is perceived as a potential threat to this cultural norm, because people believe that for Islam there is no separation between politics and religion.

In several European countries, the public expressions of Islamic identity clashes with the neutrality of the public space. Islam is by nature a religion that permeates all aspects of its adherents' lives, both in the public and the private spheres. In France, where the concept of *laïcité* shapes contemporary policy about the place of religion in public life, the consensus in the media in 2004 was that *laïcité* was in peril and that Islam was the cause.[21] The discussions in several European countries among politicians and civilians on the allowance of headscarves reveal societies struggling to reconcile a new social reality with a set of relatively consistent secular

Austin Cline, "Secularism vs Secularization: What's the Difference? Why Do People Confuse Them?" About.com., http://atheism.about.com/od/secularismseparation/a/Secularization.htm (accessed April 14, 2009) Austin Cline, Regional Director for the Council for Secular Humanism, writes: Thus, the difference between secularism and secularization is that secularism is more of a philosophical position about the way things should

[21] John R. Bowen, *Why the French don't like the Headscarves: Islam, the State and Public Space* (Princeton, New Jersey: Princeton University Press, 2006), 31.

values. In their book *Integrating Islam: Religious and Political Challenges in Contemporary France,* Jonathan Laurence, assistant professor of political science at Boston College) and Justin Vaisse French historian, adjunct professor at Sciences-Po (Paris) discuss several aspects of Islam in France. They point out that "in France the debates and the anxieties about the headscarves are about fears that the emergence of a public Islam challenges the particular institutions that guarantee life together in the Republic—a public space from which ethnic, religious and other characteristics are erased."[22]

People who fear Europe becoming *Eurabia* consider the space given to Muslims to practice their religion and to live in accordance with their values examples of the Islamization of Europe.[23]

Islam: A Threat to the Freedom of Speech?

Another area that seems to point to the growing influence of Islam in Europe and which is used to support a *Eurabia* scenario is the discussion regarding the freedom of speech. Several incidents in Europe, such as the publication of Salman Rushdie's book *The Satanic Verses*, the publication of controversial cartoons of Mohammed in a Danish newspaper, and the implementations of laws to forbid hatred on religious grounds indicate that the presence of Islam in Europe has stirred up the discussion on what the value of free speech means.

[22] Jonathan Laurence and Justin Vaisse, *Integrating Islam: Religious and Political Challenges in Contemporary France* (Washington, DC: Brookings Institute, 2006), 164.

[23] Hans Holtrop, a Dutch Christian, in an e-mail,entitled "Europa is bezig zich in een hoog tempo te onderwerpen aan de Islam" (Europe is Islamizing in a rapid speed) on September 9, 2008 sent to all Christian organizations and institutions in the Netherlands in September 2008 refers to the following as examples of how Europe submits to Islam: Muslim women asking to be exempt from lessons in sports and biology, that swimming pools have special openings hours for Muslims, that Muslim have successfully demanded that Christmas celebrations will no longer take place at primary schools, that Muslims demand rooms to pray at Europe's universities, that Muslims demand a change in our history books to include their history etc.

Some believe that the religious demands of Muslims to not be offended or insulted clashes with the value of free expression of speech.[24] It could point to a clash between the liberal Western mindset where the mind rules supreme and nothing is sacred and of the integral nature of Islam to Muslim ways of life.[25] One might also consider it a clash of two important values: a) freedom of expression and b) respect for the religious sensibilities of others. The question that comes up is whether or not it is a democratic right to take an argument to the point where somebody is offended by what we say.[26]

People like Rushdie, who believe that freedom of speech should not be used to stir up *racial* hate, think that this same freedom of speech gives them the democratic right to stir up *religious* hate. He seems to ignore that for many people religion is not just a set of intellectual beliefs, but a way of life.[27] Christians should be able to identify with Muslims in this respect. Perhaps Christians in Europe

[24] Salman Rushdie, "Defend The Right To Be Offended," *Open Democracy*, http://www.opendemocracy.net/faith-europe_islam/article_2331.jsp#/ (accessed June 5, 2008). Rushdie believes that this value comes under threat because of religious demands made by Muslims that people do not offend or insult them because of their religious convictions.

[25] Sarah Lindon, "Words On Images: The Cartoon Controversy," *Open Democracy*, http://www.opendemocracy.net/faith-europe_islam/article_2331.jsp#/ (accessed June 5, 2008).

[26] Salman Rushdie, "Defend The Right To Be Offended," *Open Democracy*, http://www.opendemocracy.net/faith-europe_islam/article_2331.jsp#/ (accessed June 5, 2008). According to Rushdie "you never personalize, but you have absolutely no respect for people's opinions. You are never rude to the person, but you can be savagely rude about what the person thinks."

[27] Shakira Hussein, "They Do Not Villfy Our Ideas, They Vilify Us: A Reply To Salman Rushdie," *Open Democracy*, http://www.opendemocracy.net/faith-multicultarism/article_2349.jsp#/ (accessed June 8, 2008). Hussein,writes: "Racial hatred is increasingly being recoded in religious terms, and frankly I don't think it is our 'ideas' that are at issue much of the time. Committed atheists are subjected to Islamophobia along with devout believers on the basis of their Arabic names or 'middle-eastern appearance'. Nor is religious identity simply about our 'ideas' in any abstract sense. It's about the community to which we belong, our families, the significance of certain days, places, or events."

have become too accustomed to having their religious convictions offended by their environment and may have actually helped the process of the erosion of free speech instead of helping people practice a form of self-censorship when using their right of freedom of speech.[28] At the same time, Muslims in Europe will have to understand that freedom of expression is a value that is important to Europeans. Muslim coming from countries where freedom of speech is not a right must take some time to adjust to this difference.

Islamic Rejection of Europe

Those who expect *Eurabia* point out that Muslims reject Europe and seek to destabilize societies through violence and terrorism in name of Islam. Although many young Muslims and intellectuals are actively looking for a way to live in harmony with their faith while fully participating in European society, one should not be blind to the fact that there also are Muslims who reject Europe. Such rejection sometimes grows out of fear, which results in another phobia.[29] There is a perception among Muslims that Western culture is decadent and debased. This perception is fueled by regular statements in the Muslim media that reflect and often exaggerate moral decay in Western societies.

[28] Ibid.

[29] Michael Ancram, "Clash or Dialogue of Civilisations?" (speech, Oxford Centre for Islamic Studies, May 16, 2003) Michael Ancram, http://www.michaelancram.com/sp_display.aspx?id=69 (accessed April 13, 2009). Ancram, UK member of Parliament, refers to 'westoxification' and said: "Fear is at the core. Fear on each side of being dominated by the other. Not the desire to conquer each other, but the fear of being overwhelmed and run by the other... So I believe it is between Islamic Fundamentalists and the West. Their mindset is not one of conquest but of fear. They fear what has been called 'Westoxification'. The fear of 'Westoxification' is the fear that another culture, in this case that of 'the West' can seduce followers of other cultures or ways of life, in this case followers of Islam, away from their Faith and the way of life which goes with it. 'Westoxification' is a particularly apposite term for it is both addictive and seductive, and yet at the same toxic."

This negative stereotyping of the West has been termed *Westophobia.*[30] Although the sentiment might be real, the term *Westophobia* is not as widely used as *Islamophobia.* One definition given of *Westophobia* is that "*Westophobia* refers to entrenched and endemically hostile attitudes to the West and to perceived cultural traits of the West."[31] Another term which seems to reflect the same sentiment and might be a synonym is *Occidentalism.* Zadar, a visiting Professor of Postcolonial Studies of City University in London and author of over forty books on various aspects of Islam, believes that *Occidentalism* seems poised to become the dominant discourse of the future.[32] Riddell and Cotterell mention the following causes for antipathy toward the West among the Muslim masses:

1) The Israeli-Palestinian conflict;
2) United Nations sanctions against Iraq;
3) American military presence in Saudi Arabia;
4) Negative stereotyping of non-Muslims in Islamic sacred scripture;
5) The legacy of history;
6) Globalization;
7) Westophobia in Muslim media;
8) Conspiracy theorizing.[33]

In Europe one also finds extreme Islamists who have come to Europe to use the freedom here to fight against what they see as

[30] George Carey, "The Cross and the Crescent (The Clash of Faiths in an Age of Secularism)," September 18, 2006, The Beach Lecture, Newbold College, Bracknell. http://www.glcarey.co.uk/Speeches/2006/Cross%20and%20Crescent.html?.html (accessed April 14, 2009). Carey, former Archbishop of Canterbury, stated that "in recent years a deep-seated Westophobia has developed in the Muslim world."

[31] Peter G Riddell & Peter Cotterell, *Islam in Context: past, present and future* (Grand Rapids, MI: Baker Academic, 2004 (second edition), 160.

[32] Ziauddin Zadar, "Why do they hate us?" review of *Occidentalism: A Short History of Anti-Westernism*, by Buruma, Ian, *New Statesman* (October 4 2004).

[33] Riddell & Cotterell, 160.

violations of the Islamic truth.[34] Some believe they can't participate in Western societies and seek to establish a *Khalifat* in Europe.[35] Although they are fringe groups at the moment, one should be aware that the lack of integration of Muslims has the potential to foster social and political instability and conflict.[36] Failure on the part of the society to help Muslims integrate into society leads to alienated and marginalized Muslims who are vulnerable to extreme Islamists.[37]

It is important to distinguish between radical Islamists[38] and conservative Muslims, because conservative Muslims interpret the *Qu'ran* conservatively without becoming *jihadic* warriors.[39] One example of this last group is the Muslim Brothers who are an ac-

[34] Robert Leiken, "Europe's Angry Muslims," *Foreign Affairs* 84, no. 4 (July/August 2005). Leiken warns for first-generation jihadists who have migrated to Europe expressly to carry out jihad. He describes them as aliens, typically asylum seekers or students, who gained refuge in liberal Europe from crackdowns against Islamists in the Middle East. Among them are radical imams, often on stipends from Saudi Arabia, who open their mosques to terrorist recruiters and serve as messengers for or spiritual fathers to jihadist networks.

[35] Ramadan, *Western Muslims*, 24–27.Ramadan discusses six various trends of thought within Islam and he admits that some of these streams cannot conceive of participating in Western societies (e.g. the scholastic traditionalism of the *Taliban* and *Tabligh- I Jamaat*) or refuse any kind of involvement in a space that is considered non-Islamic (e. g. *Salafi Literalism*) Others, like political literalist salafism, which in Europe is found among the *Hizb al-Tahrir* and *Al-Muhajirun* wed a literal reading of the Texts with a political connotation concerning the management of power, the caliphate, authority, law. He also points out that *Salafi* reformist thought, that adopts a reading of the sources that is based on the purpose and intentions of the law and jurisprudence, is very widespread in the West.

[36] Pauly 167, 168. Pauly gives three examples in which such conflicts are manifested in contemporary Western Europe: a) the above-average crime rates in urban districts in which Islamic communities are situated; b) the confrontations between younger generations of Muslims and the police that periodically escalate into large-scale riots; c) the rising support for far-right political parties.

[37] Leiken, "Europe's Angry Muslims". Leiken states that "the social malaise felt by Muslims in the suburbs of major cities can turn into extremism and terrorism."

[38] Klausen, 46. Klausen finds that the new radical Islamist groups combine a global utopianism with a paranoid conception of power.

[39] Klausen, 45. Klausen suggests that these people should be described as neo-orthodox.

tivist movement with an enlightened conservatism and a devoutly religious outlook that continues to attract young educated Muslims.[40]

While failure to integrate Muslims could lead to a growth of radical Islam in Europe, integrating Muslims in European societies and helping them understand and embrace both explicitly and implicitly European values can also lead to tensions within the Muslim community. Muslim men may feel threatened by the loss of social control over Muslim women who are drawn to modern individualistic values and forms of emancipation as a result of their public education.[41]

Euro-Islam

Introduction

Euro-Islam conceptually expects that Islam will be Europeanized and Islamic values are compatible with those of Europe, and the two will exist side by side. The concept of *Euro-Islam* was introduced in 1992 by Bassam Tibi, a Syrian born Muslim and a German citizen. He is a political scientist and professor of International Relations at Gottingen University in Germany, and a professor at Cornell University. He is an advocate of reforming Islam. *Euro-Islam*, then, is the idea that Muslim migrants in Europe bring their identity into harmony with Europe and its cultural system. Tibi explains his concept of *Euro-Islam* as an "Europeanization of Islam."[42]

[40] Cesari, *Islam and Democracy*, 143. Cesari points out that this movement "wants to reconcile the exigencies of Islam with secular life without losing their soul."

[41] Fadela Amera and Sylvie Zappi, *Breaking the Silence* (: California University Press, 2006), 25. Helen Harden Chenut, who translated Amara's book and wrote an introduction to it, states: "There is little doubt that the message of female emancipation and individual rights clashes overtly with fundamentalist assertion of religious and patriarchal authority."

[42] Bassam Tibi, "Europeanisation, Not Islamisation," Sign and Sight.com http://www.signandsight.com/features/1258.html. (accessed December 28, 2008).

Another *Euro-Islam* advocate is Tarik Ramadan, a Swiss Muslim academic whose views on Islam reflect a reformist perspective. Ramadan calls for creating a new European-Muslim identity and encourages Muslims to participate in Europe's social and cultural life. He calls for Muslims to essentially conform to European culture, but maintain Muslim ethics. Ramadan asserts that Islamic principles be separated from their cultures of origin and anchor them in the cultural reality of Western Europe.[43]

Islam's Adaptation to Europe

The rapid growth in the number of Islamic centers more than six thousand in Western Europe in the past three decades are accompanied by an increase in Muslim funeral parlors, *halal* butcher shops, Islamic schools, etc. serves as a clear indication that Islam has begun to establish itself in the democratic and secularized context of Europe. Ramadan believes that Europe is currently living through a silent revolution in Muslim communities in the West in which more and more young people and intellectuals are actively looking for a way to live in harmony with their faith while participating in the societies that are their societies, whether they like it or not.[44]

The fact that Islam is beginning to adapt to the European context can particularly be noticed in: (1) the emergence of Islamic political and civic leaders and Islamic associations; (2) changes in religious authority; (3) changes in describing Islam's status as a mi-

[43] Tariq Ramadan, *Western Muslims and the future of Islam* (Oxford: Oxford University Press, 2004), 4. Ramadan has been called Islam's 'Martin Luther' in the West for his controversial views that challenge the mainstream Islamic beliefs. He teaches theology at the University of Oxford.

[44] Ramadan, *Western Muslims,* 9. Ramadan encourages Western Muslims to go back to their sources and distinguish between what in their religion is unchangeable (*thabit*) from what is subject to change (*mutaghay-yir*).

nority culture; (4) a desire for gender equality, and (5) changes in interpreting the meaning of *shari'a*.[45]

The Emergence of Political and Civic Leaders and Associations

European Muslim leaders play an important role in the accommodation of Islam in Europe. A significant number of them are people that have in one way or another chosen to live in Europe and indicated their acceptance of European norms and institutions by engaging in civic and political life.[46] Research shows that Europe's new Muslim political elite are first generation immigrants that focus on national politics and use the national language. They are integrationists and people who consider Islam to be significant in their personal lives.[47]

Initially the religious needs of immigrants in Europe were met by the governments of Muslim countries (e.g. Morocco, Turkey, Saudi Arabia, and Algeria). They collaborated with the local European governments, but gradually European governments sought to limit foreign government influence in the practice of Islam in their countries. All European governments with sizable Muslim minorities have initiated consultations with a broad swath of Muslim religious organizations and prayer spaces, and they have pursued the

[45] In chapter 9 of her book *When Islam and Democracy meet*, Cesari mentions several other reforms, such as interfaith dialogue, the concept of democracy, the status of the Apostate and human rights.

[46] Jytte Klausen, *The Islamic Challenge: politics and religion in Western Europe* (Oxford: Oxford University Press, 2005).Jytte Klausen, Professor of Politics at Brandeis University and Research Associate at The Center for European Studies, at Harvard University, estimates there are between 1,500 and 2,000 individuals in six European countries (Sweden, Denmark, the Netherlands, Great Britain, France and Germany), who are elected or appointed leaders in a national or regional civic or political organization and who are of Muslim faith or background. She interviewed 300 of them and she portrays the results of this in her book.

[47] Klausen, 28. According to Klausen the 9/11 attacks became a catalyst for a new wave of Muslim associationalism and created the emergence of national faith-based umbrella groups or councils that focus on national political participation and that consider their support for integration as their chief objective.

domestication of Islam as well as of other major religious communities by institutionalizing church-state relations. Even in France, with the model of *laïcité* the state has been very active in their creation of the French Council on the Muslim Religion.[48]

Changes in Religious Authority

One can see a democratization of authority in Islam in Europe when compared to Islam in the native countries of the European Muslims.[49] During the pilot of the course Sharing Lives with Bible school students, which will be discussed in more detail in chapter 5, I have seen an example of this practice.

On November 21, 2008, I visited a mosque in Amsterdam, whose board consists of predominantly young people from different ethnic backgrounds and I was welcomed by the chairman of the board of the mosque, a 24-year old woman. She explicitly mentioned that the board operates independently of national or international bodies.

The changes in the structure of Islam in the West particularly affect the status of religious leaders. The bureaucratic leader, paid by or otherwise associated with the Islamic institutions of influential Muslim countries, is increasingly replaced by the community or "parochial" leader, whose activity is concentrated in the mosque or Islamic association of a particular neighborhood or city.[50]

[48] Klausen, 138. Klausen writes: "Rather than simply tolerate the existence of Islam *in* France, the government has made it a policy goals to create an Islam *of* France."

[49] Cesari, *Islam and Democracy*, 124. Cesari points out that Muslims are in the process of creating new institutions and forms of authority appropriate in their new environment.

[50] Cesari, *Islam and Democracy*, 139. Cesari believes that within the gradual restructuring of Muslim communities in the West, "the emergence of 'parochial leaders' constitutes a noteworthy phenomenon."

Islam's Status as a Minority Culture

Within the Muslim community in the West an intense debate goes on over the legal conditions connected to minority status. The main Islamic concepts in this regard are *Dar al Islam,* "House of Peace," and *Dar al Harb*, "House of War." Most Muslims in Europe consider the classical distinction between these concepts void.[51] At the moment there is no consensus about the name to be given to *Dar al Harb*. Ramadan lists some options that are used. Some prefer to use the concept of *Dar-al-Ahd,* "Abode of Treaty," or *Dar-al-Amn,* "Abode of safety." Others prefer to speak of *Dar-al-Dawa,* "Abode of Invitation to God." Others prefer the notion of *Shahada,* "Testimony," and refer to the Western countries as *Dar al-Shahada,* "Abode of Testimony."[52]

A Desire for Gender Equality

It is not hard to imagine a clash on gender issues when comparing the sexually liberal Western societies with the far more conservative societies of North Africa, Turkey, and the Middle East. Dr. Amina Wadud, an Islamic studies professor at Virginia Commonwealth University, located in Richmond, Virginia, considers gender one of the most crucial contemporary issues facing Islam and Muslims.[53] In many European countries, discussions are going on with regard to the wearing of the veil, and several countries have passed laws forbidding Muslim girls from wearing headscarves while at school. Often Islamic headscarves are seen in a negative light and considered to be a symbol of mounting Islam-

[51] Ramadan, *Western Muslims,* 66. After giving some details about the debates that have gone on about these concepts, Ramadan concludes that these concepts seem "neither operational nor relevant in our time."

[52] Ramadan, *Western Muslims*, 75.

[53] Amina Wadud, *Inside the Gender Jihad: Women's Reform in Islam* (Oxford: One World Publications, 2006), 79.

ism.[54] The link is made between Muslim women wearing a scarf and the failure of Muslims to integrate into European society or between the scarf and Islam's aversion of modernism.

Developments are taking place within Islam, particularly among Western Muslims towards more gender equality. In her books and teachings, Dr. Wadud explains, defines and redefines several key concepts of Islam,[55] and reinterprets Islam and its primary sources in such a way that it no longer justifies the gender inequality and patriarchism.[56]

Dr. Wadud, a hero for some and a heretic for others, is an example of how people that are fully committed to Islam seek to reform it from within.[57]

Changed Meaning of *Shari'a*

Those who support the *Eurabia* scenario are afraid that in the near future *shari'a* law (the body of Islamic religious law) will be operative throughout Europe. By means of a questionnaire I found that 64 percent of the Christian respondents agreed or didn't ex-

[54] Bowen, 98. Bowen points out that in France "the scarves were seen as the key to a whole host of problems. Ban the scarves and things will, somehow, get better: boys will stop harassing girls, Islamists will stop harassing secular Muslims, and teachers will get more respect."

[55] For example *tawhid* (the unicity of God); *khalifah* (moral agent); *taqwa* (moral consciousness).

[56] Wadud, 88. She believes that "an alternative interpretation of the Qur'an from a female-inclusive perspective is instrumental in reform movements in modern Muslim societies."

[57] Wadud has been the subject of much debate and Muslim juristic discourse. In August 1994, she delivered a Friday sermon in a mosque in Cape Town, South Africa. At the time, this was largely unheard of in the Muslim world. As a result, there were attempts by some Muslims to have her removed from her position at the university. There has been objection and some support from Muslims around the world to Wadud's imamate. In spite of the criticism, Wadud has continued her speaking engagements, and has continued to lead mixed-gender Friday prayer services. In 2005, she was invited to lead a congregation of about thirty people in Barcelona, Spain and also in 2005 she led a Friday prayer of over 100 male and female Muslims in New York

plicitly disagree with the statement "For Muslims jihad means to subjugate foreign lands and people."[58]

In this light is it important to notice that Muslims in Europe seek to define their identity within the framework of European legal orders and to apply the *shari'a* law within the European contexts. The *shari'a* contains religious as well as legal norms of Islam. It is constructed from the *Qur'an* and the *Sunnah* and developed in the context of a Muslim majority situation. Muslims in Europe are in the process of defining which aspects of it are also applicable in the European context. Muslim scholars, such as Tarik Ramadan, differentiate between the universal principles, which remain the same through the ages and the practice of these principles, which are relative at a given moment in history.[59] Mathias Rohe, judge of the Court of Appeal in Nürenberg, Germany sees a "deterritorialization" regarding the non-legal parts of the *shari'a*.

> The provisions, the legal consequences of which can only be enforced with the help of a state sanction system, remain territorially connected to the exercising of Islamic state power. All other provisions are principally universal and are therefore also open for application and further development within the regional environment.[60]

Sometimes, in specific cases, Muslim jurists must determine how a Muslim can adapt to the Western context.[61] These rulings point to the development of a European *shari'a*. This situation is exemplified by some of the Islamic institutions that have been es-

[58] For more information, see chapter 5 and Appendix D.

[59] Tariq Ramadan, *Western Muslims*, 95. Ramadan believes that to apply the *shari'a* for Muslim citizens or residents in the West means explicitly to respect that legal and constitutional framework of the country of which they are citizens."

[60] Matthias Rohe, *Muslim Minorities and the Law in Europe—Changes and Challenges* (New Delhi: GM Publications, 2007), 53. In this book Rohe discusses whether and to which extent norms of the *shari'a* can be applied in Europe.

[61] Ramadan, *Western Muslims*, 97. Ramadan points out that sometimes Muslims need to object to certain matters that are required of them, by pointing to the conscience cause. At other times the latitude of the national constitution needs to be constrained by the personal choice of a Muslim in order to live in accordance with their faith.

tablished, such as the Islamic Shari'a Council in England (*Angrezi Shari'at*),[62] and the European Council for Expert Opinions and Studies (also called the European Council for Fatwa and Research).[63] Also of importance is the Islamic Charta of the German Central Council of Muslims, because in this organization for the first time organized Muslims formulated their position about the adherence to Islam as well as to European citizenship.[64]

In the areas of family law and laws of succession, the existing European legal system gives space for the possibility of applying Islamic laws.[65] In some European countries, the legislator has made legal provisions for defined groups.[66] Other areas in which Muslims have a legal opportunity to apply their own laws are within

[62] Rohe, 54. The Council, established in 1980, is responsible for mediation particularly in the area of the law on a person's legal status (matters relating to marriage, divorce). Decisions by the Council which cannot be challenged, can be enforced by state courts.

[63] European Council for Fatwa and Research, *First collection of Fatwas* (Cairo: Islamic INC, 1999). Founded in 1997. it has 30 members, 22 of whom live in Europe, the rest in the Arab world. By publishing its expert opinions the Council aims at providing emigrated Muslims with advice regarding problems they are faced with in everyday life. Since 1999, the Council meets every year and presents a volume containing its expert opinions in Arabic. Forty three of their opinions (*fatwahs*) that came out of their first two meetings are collected in English in "First collection of Fatwahs". These opinions deal with the following topics: mission/general questions of faith; ritual purity and prayer; questions concerning property; gainful employment and housekeeping; marriage and divorce; family and the Muslim household; food; character and tradition; general.

[64] Rohe, 143. This Islamic Charta made in 2002 stressed that Muslims are content with the harmonious system of secularism and religious freedom provided by the Constitution and that they don't intend to create 'a state of God'. In some articles it is pointed out that Muslims willingly accept the German legal order including the rights of women to take place in elections, the right to change religion and the provision of German Family Laws, the Law of Inheritance and Procedural Law.

[65] Rohe, 117. Rohe points out that the application of Islamic family law—within the limits of public policy—has become everyday business in German courts. Islamic law has largely preserved its dominant position especially within the area of personal status (marital and family law). However, the application of such provisions must comply with the rules of the German public policy.

[66] Rohe, 20. For example, in its new Personal Status Law, 1992, Spain has recognized the Islamic formal way of contracting a marriage as an option.

the framework of optional civil law and economic contracts, such as mortgages.[67]

Assessing the Two Scenarios

The bulk of Muslims in Europe arrived in the 1960s as guest workers with the idea of making money and returning home to their families. In the 1980s it became clear that that was not to be. Instead, women and children and other relatives joined the husbands and Islam took root in Europe. Gradually, Muslims, governments, and European citizens realized that they have a future together. How this future will look is not yet clear. What is clear is that adjustments have to be made by both Muslims and the European societies.

As has been shown earlier there are many who believe that Europe will do most of the adjusting resulting in Europe becoming *Eurabia*. They seem to assume that Islam will be immune to the pressure of secularization. Philip Jenkins, who in his book *God's Continent, Christianity, Islam and Europe's Religious Crisis*, argues against a *Eurabia* scenario, points out that

> both Christianity and Islam face real difficulties in surviving within Europe's secular cultural ambience in anything like their familiar historic forms. But instead of fading away, both have adapted to Eurosecularity and there are continuing to adapt. The fate of Islam in cotemporary Europe must be understood in the wider religious context, so that both Islam and Christianity are considered together in terms of maintaining their hold on believers, and in their relationship with the secular order.[68]

Many Muslims in Europe face the challenge of how to maintain a spiritual life in a modern secular society. According to Cesari, the

[67] Rohe, 23. In the UK a special concept of "Islamic mortgages" was developed, which allows Muslims willing to purchase chattel to avoid conflicts with provisions concerning *riba* (when paying interest on 'normal' mortgages.

[68] Jenkins, 3.

greatest problem Muslims in Europe have is "how to transfer legitimacy from the Muslim world to the West? How to transfer theology from the Muslim world to the Western world?"[69]

Those who believe we are heading for *Eurabia* point out that hard-core Islam is incapable of modernity and that there is no such thing as a moderate Islam. Professor Mahmood Mamdani, President of the Council for Development of Social Research in Africa (CODESRIA) Dakar, Senegal argues that those people, who believe that Islam is incapable of modernity, fail to distinguish between fundamentalism as a religious identity and a political identity that uses a religious idiom, such as political Islam.[70]

Earlier in this chapter I demonstrated that Islamic scholars work are working towards creating a *Euro-Islam* that is both compatible with their own religious sources and their lives in Western Europe.[71] This process is far from complete and new *fatwa's* have to be produced for those who want to be faithful Muslims in a secular society. In the meantime there might be some confusion and uncertainty,[72] or even conflict between Muslims who interpret Islamic values and the *Qur'anic* truths differently and those that decide to

[69] Cesari, *Islam and Democracy*, 154.

[70] Mahmood Mamdani, *Good Muslim, Bad Muslim* (New York: Pantheon Books, 2004), 17. In this book Mamdani. is critical of those who consider Islamic civilization as if it were a veneer with its essence an unchanging doctrine in which Muslims are said to take refuge in times of crisis and he is also critical of those who divide the Islamic community between good and bad Muslims, whereby good Muslims are modern, secular and Westernized, but bad Muslims are doctrinal, antimodern, and virulent.

[71] Rohe, 156. Rohe writes that the declarations and opinions formulated by European Muslim organizations make clear that a clash of civilizations between Islam in general and western values is far from reality.

[72] Cesari, *Islam and Democracy*, 154, 155. Cesari points out that there still is a lot of uncertainty surrounding the teaching of Islam in a European context and she mentions several consequences: the widespread tendency in contemporary Islam to categorize everything as either haram or halal; schools of jurisprudence (hanafite, malekite, shafi'ite, hanbalite) are often regarded with suspicion, and sometimes wholly rejected and the differences between Sunni and Shiite Islam tend to be minimized.

leave Islam altogether and speak critically about it.[73] In fact, some element of conflict seems inevitable as Jenkins points out:

> In the last forty years, some millions of Africans and Asians have moved from traditional-minded societies dominated by Islam to European nations that differ from them in virtually every basic assumption about social arrangements and political structures, and that were themselves making an epochal transition in their own sexual mores. Against such a background, it is inconceivable that conflicts should not have erupted. Rather than despairing or seeing culture clashes as irreconcilable, we might rather be impressed at just how much convergences of values and beliefs has occurred.[74]

Based on the readings and research as presented in this chapter, I conclude that a *Euro-Islam* scenario is more likely than a *Eurabian* scenario. Nevertheless, even if the majority of Muslims are willing to find their place in Europe, they do not wholeheartedly embrace all Western values, particularly in the area of family and personal morality. What many Muslim clerics describe as the Muslim point of view in regard to family or moral issues is largely a means of keeping their distance from the cultural underpinnings of the West, and thus functions as an implicit critique of Western democracy.[75]

Despite the fact that there are a remarkable number of cases concerning Islamic legal orders, which do not cause any problems in European legal practice, the potential of conflicting legal principles between Islam-orientated rules and those of the European legal order is considerable.[76]

[73] E. g. former Dutch-Somali MP and former Muslim, Ayaan Hirsi Ali, who made the film *Submission* exposing the way Islam treats women; and former Muslim, Iranian-born Dutchman Ehsan Jami, who in December 2008 made a film "An interview with Muhammad," in which he critically looks at the life and teachings of Muhammed.

[74] Jenkins, 204.

[75] Cesari, *Islam and Democracy*, 157. Cesari writes that the internalization of democratic values by some Muslims, and Muslim leaders in particular, is colored by a good deal of skepticism for the universality of certain principles.

[76] Rohe, 117.Rohe believes that conflicts mainly arise from the application of provisions reflecting classical Islamic Law, which preserve a strict separation between the sexes with respect to their social roles and tasks.

Although the *Euro-Islam* scenario is more likely to become reality than the *Eurabia* scenario, the outcome is not only dependent upon the Muslims themselves. The outcome is dependent upon whether or not Muslims manage to bring Europe and Islam in harmony with each other and whether European governments and citizens, including Christians, are willing to create space for Islam and Muslims to find their place in Europe.

Governments are willing to develop programs and policies to help Muslims socially, culturally, and religiously find their place in Europe. But how will these programs work for the rank and file citizens? The September 11 attacks and the suicide attacks in Europe only exacerbated the predominantly negative and fearful attitude of Europeans towards Islam and Muslims.

Also among Christians in Europe, Islam and Muslims are looked at in a negative light. Fear, prejudice, and suspicion of Islam and Muslims are real, and seem to be "fuelled" every time another incident takes place involving Muslims. People often talk about Islam in an abstract way, instead of seeking to build meaningful relations with their Muslim neighbours. They only look at the Islamic textbooks instead of how individual Muslims practice their faith.

The phrase that best characterizes how Europeans, including Christians, generally deal with the growing visibility of Islam in Europe, is one that is used by Bowen in his book *Why the French don't like the Headscarves*, namely *cold tolerance*.[77] Such cold tolerance might be the result of an attitude of fear, which will be looked at in the next chapter.

[77] Bowen, 120.

Chapter Two
Dealing with Fear of Islam

Introduction

In Europe there is a widespread tendency to conflate one's perspective on Islam as an international political force with one's perspective on the ordinary Muslims living as a minority population in the countries of the West. Islam is seen as the enemy outside and the enemy within. This attitude came to be called *Islamophobia*.

Islamophobia continues to remain strong in Europe and is expressed in public with increasing frequency. The thesis of this chapter is that Christians should be agents of change rather than being molded by the societies in which they live.

In this chapter I researched some features of *Islamophobia* and its consequences and described how Christians not only tend to share in the *Islamophobia* in Europe but also have some specific perceptions which may increase their fear of Islam.

I wrote a theological assessment of the roots of fear, pointing out that fear is associated with the fallenness of humanity and summarized problematic attitudes through Volf's category of *exclusion*.[1] I then examined ways forward, using Volf's metaphor of *embrace* and the theological category of *grace* which will lead one to considering the cross as a model for relationships with Muslims.

[1] Miroslav Volf, *Exclusion and Embrace* (Nashville, US: Abingdon Press, 1996). In this book Kroatian theologian Miroslav Volf looks in a theological way at ethnic and cultural conflicts. Volf's book is set against the background of the inter-ethnic problems in the Balkans. This dissertation uses Volfs' metaphors of *exclusion* and *embrace* to reflect on the fear of Christians for Muslims and how to overcome and change this.

Islamophobia in Europe

Across Europe there is a prevalent attitude towards Islam that is described as *Islamophobia*. Since 1991 the term *Islamophobia*[2] has been used widely to describe the attitude of fear and hatred of Muslim people and Islam as a religion.[3]

Islamophobia is defined in different ways such as: "fear or suspicion of Islam, Muslims, and matters pertaining to them,"[4] "a useful shorthand way of referring to dread or hatred of Islam—and therefore, to fear or dislike of all or most Muslims,"[5] or "a powerful or an irrational fear or dislike of the Islamic faith and its believers by non Muslims, resulting in stereotyping, prejudice, discrimination and insults which are often accompanied by acts of hatred and discrimination against followers of the Islamic faith"[6] Despite its wide use, the concept *Islamophobia* has not been without controversy. The term has been criticized by a number of commentators for its loose definition and broad application and its use remains a contested issue. Some prefer to replace the word *Islamophobia* with "anti-

[2] The Oxford English Dictionary refers to the periodical *Insight* of 4th February 1991 as the first use of 'Islamophobia'.

[3] The term features in several reports and documents of the European Monitoring Centre on Racism and Xenophobia (EUMC). The Organisation of the Islamic Conference (OIC), the second largest inter-governmental organization after the United Nations and considered the collective voice of the Muslim world, set up an observatory on *Islamophobia* in 2005 to monitor and document activities perceived as Islamophobic around the world. In 2005, The website *Islamophobia Watch (www.islamophobia-watch.com)* was initiated to document material in the public domain which advocates a fear and hatred of the Muslim peoples of the world and Islam as a religion. The Islamic Human Rights Commission hands out "Islamophobe of the year" awards (www.ihrc.org).

[4] Ingrid Ramberg, "Islamophobia And Its Consequences On Young People," Eycb, June, 2004, http://eych.coe.int/eycbwwwroot/HRE/eng/documents/Islamophobia%20report/Islamophobia%final%ENG.pdf. (accessed April 14, 2009).

[5] The Runnymede Trust, *Islamophobia: A Challenge for Us All* (London: The Runnymede Trust, 1997), 4.

[6] Organization of the Islamic Conference, "First Annual Report On Islamophobia," *Permanent Mission Of The Organization Of The Islamic Conference*, 2007, http://www.oic-un.org/reports.asp/ (accessed April 14, 2009).

Islamic racism"[7] Some believe the more accurate term is "anti-Muslimism."[8] Some call it "a challenge for us all,"[9] "a violation of human rights and a threat to social cohesion,"[10] "so widespread that it may be more prevalent and dominant than racial abuse,"[11] one of the major issues facing present day international relations."[12] Others refer to it as "a myth"[13] or denounce it as "a wretched concept that confuses criticism of Islam as a religion and stigmatization of those who believe in it."[14] While some believe that has a grip upon Europe,[15] others believe that "promoters of the *Islamophobia* concept habitually exaggerate the problem."[16]

[7] Al-Maktabi, "Islamophobia," *Salaam*, http://www.salaam.co.uk/maktabi/islamophobia.html. (accessed April 14, 2009). The author believes *Islamophobia* combines the elements of dislike of a religion.

[8] Fred Halliday, "Islamophobia Reconsidered," *Ethnic and Racial Studies* 22, no.5 (September 1999): 892–902. According to Halliday, the enemy is not a faith or a culture, but a people.

[9] The Runnymede Trust, in the title of their booklet: *Islamophobia: A Challenge for Us All* London: The Runnymede Trust, 1997)

[10] Ingrid Ramberg, "Islamophobia and its consequences on Young People," Seminar Report of European Youth Centre Budapest, June 1–6, 2004. EYCB, http://eycb.coe.int/eycbwwwroot/HRE/eng/documents/Islamophobia%20report/Islamophobia%20final%20ENG.pdf (accessed, April 14, 2009).

[11] Necmi Sadikoglu, ","speech delivered to International Conference on Islamophobia, December 8, 2007, Istanbul. http://www.oicun.org/articles/120/1/International-Conference-on-Islamophobia-OIC-SG-Statement-Dec-2007/1.html (accessed April 14, 2009).

[12] Organization of the Islamic Conference "The updated report of the OIC Observatory on Islamophobia to the 35th Session of the Council of Foreign Ministers for the period of May 2007-May 2008" Permanent Mission of the Organization of the Islamic Conference, http://www.oic-un.org/reports.asp#Reports (accessed April 14, 2009).

[13] Kenan Malik, "Islamophobia Myth," *Prospect*, http://www.prospect-magazine.co.uk/article_details.php?id=6679/ (accessed April 14, 2009).

[14] BBC News. "Writers statement on cartoons." BBC News. http://news.bbc.co.uk/2/hi/europe/4764730.stm (accessed April 14, 2009).

[15] Stephen Castle, "Islamophobia Takes A Grip Across Europe," *The Independent*, http://www.independent.co.uk/news/europ/islamophobia-takes-a-grip-across-europe-429021.html. (accessed April 14,2009).

[16] Daniel Pipes. "Islamophobia?" New York Sun. http://www.danielpipes.org/3075/islamophobia (accessed April 14, 2009).

Although the term is sometimes referred to as unfounded hostility or irrational fear[17] those who are considered Islamophobes state that their fear is far from irrational or unfounded and that it is not fear of Islam in general, but a fear of radical Islam.[18]

Features of Islamophobia in Europe

In 1996 The Runnymede Trust, a UK based independent research and policy agency, set up the Commission on British Muslims and Islamophobia, under the chairmanship of Professor Gordon Conway of the University of Sussex. In August 1997 this Commission produced their final report, *Islamophobia: A Challenge for Us All*. This was the first time that the subject of *Islamophobia* had been comprehensively tackled in relation to Muslims in the United Kingdom. This document continues to play an important role in discussions on *Islamophobia*, not just in the UK, but also elsewhere in Europe. The report *Islamophobia: A challenge for Us All*, makes a link between *Islamophobia* and having a

[17] The Runnymede Trust writes that "the term Islamophobia refers to *unfounded* hostility towards Islam.", *Islamophobia: A Challenge for Us All*, 4. The website www.islamophobia.org calls it an "*irrational*" fear or prejudice towards islam and Muslims.

[18] Daniel Pipes, who has been called "the world's most prominent ant-Muslim hatemonger" http://www.mereislam.info/labels/Holocaust.html but who prefers to call himself an "Islamism-ophobe" writes that "Islamophobia deceptively conflates two distinct phenomena: fear of Islam and fear of radical Islam." http://www.danielpipes.org/article/3075

Another so-called Islamophobe, Bat Ye'or gives ample justification for her point of view. In her book *Eurabia: The Euro-Arab Axis* is very suspicious of the growth of Islam in Europe and is convinced that Europe is in the process of becoming Eurabia, citing many articles, reports, particularly pointing to the way Islam has interpreted jihad.

Robert Spencer, director of Jihad Watch, who is called "an inveterate Islam-hater," writes he does not hate Muslims, but that he mainly calls attention to the roots and goals of jihad violence. http://www.jihadwatch.org/spencer/

Paty Santi believes that "fear of the fanatics of Islam is far from irrational. Being afraid... after the innumerable acts of violence, terror and depravity committed in the name of Allah is not exaggerated; not inexplicable; and most certainly not illogical." http://drsanity.blogspot.com/

"closed view" of Islam. They give the following eight characteristics of such a closed view:[19]

1) Islam is seen as monolithic and static rather than diverse and dynamic. People with closed views of Islam are insensitive to the differences and variations within the world of Islam and picture Islam as intolerant of internal pluralism, ignoring the debates that go on among Muslims on matters like human rights, relationship with secularism etc.
2) Islam is seen as other and separate rather than as similar and independent. People with closed views of Islam consider Islam as hermetically sealed off from the rest of the world, with no common roots and no borrowing or mixing in either direction.
3) Islam is seen as inferior not different. People with closed views of Islam often consider Muslims as primitive, violent, irrational, scheming, disorganized, and oppressive, while they themselves are civilized, reasonable, generous, efficient, sophisticated and enlightened. [20]
4) Islam is seen as the enemy not as a partner. People with closed views see Islam as violent and aggressive, firmly committed to barbaric terrorism, and implacably hostile to the non-Muslim world.
5) Muslims are seen as manipulative not as sincere. People with closed views frequently consider that Muslims use their reli-

[19] Although this is not the only way of analyzing the problem of *Islamophobia*, these characteristics are included in this dissertation because they still play an important role on how people define Islamophobia in Europe. For example, when defining *Islamophobia* in their document *Muslims in the European Union—Discrimination and Islamophobia* (2006), the European Monitoring Centre for Racism and Xenophobia (EUMC) writes that an "important reference point are the eight features attributed to Islamophobia in the 1997 publication by the UK-based NGO the Runnymede Trust 'Islamophobia: A Challenge for Us All'." (61).

[20] In a questionnaire among Christians, I did in November 2008, only 27 percent states that they believe that Muslims' civilization is as good and high as western civilization For more information, see chapter 5 and appendix D.

gion for strategic, political, and military advantage rather than as a religious faith and as a way of life.[21]

6) Racial discrimination against Muslims is defended rather than challenged. A closed view of Islam has the effect of justifying racism, and anti-immigrant prejudice.
7) Muslim criticism of "the West" are rejected and not considered. A closed view of Islam frequently dismisses criticisms which Muslims make of western liberalism, modernity and secularism, and considers them not worthy for debate.
8) Anti-Muslim discourse is seen as natural not as problematic. Islamophobic discourse which is sometimes blatant and often subtle and coded, is part of the fabric of everyday life in many countries in Europe.

Fear of Islam and Muslims Among Christians in Europe

From the questionnaires I did, I've discovered that often Christians share a "closed" view of Islam with their fellow Europeans and the characteristics of it mentioned above. In addition I can identify the following fear-raising factors that cause many Christians in Europe to have a negative attitude towards Muslims and Islam.

Persecution of Christians

In an online symposium of FrontPage Magazine, dated October 10, 2003, managing editor Jamie Glazov discussed the issue of The Muslim Persecution of Christians with Bat Ye'or, Paul Marshal

[21] In a questionnaire among Christians I did in November 2008, 70 percent do not explicitly disagree with the statement that Muslims do not show their real face until they are a majority, and 43 percent of respondents are not willing to trust Muslims, and only 20 percent wholeheartedly want to give Muslims the benefit of the doubtFor more information, see chapter 5 and appendix D.

and Habib Malik and concluded that the Muslim persecution of Christians is clearly a widespread and horrifying phenomenon.[22]

In the World Watch List, a list of the top fifty worst persecuting countries in the world published annually by the Christian organization Open Doors Islam is the majority religion in six of the top ten worst persecuting countries: Saudi Arabia, Iran, Maldives, Afghanistan, Yemen, and Uzbekistan.[23]

Christians living in countries dominated by Islam (e. g. Nigeria, Egypt, Pakistan and Indonesia) often testify of the difficulties they face from the hands of Islamic authorities or Muslims in their cities or villages. Such difficulties vary from persecution, verbal assaults, destroying property, inability to attend a certain university, finding a certain job.[24] The difficulties faced by those who converted from Islam to Christianity can be worse and even lead to their murder.[25]

Christians who do not experience these acts of persecution themselves hear about them through organizations such as Open

[22] Jamie Glazov, "Symposium:the Muslim Persecution Of Christians," *Frontpage-magazine*, http://www.frontpagemag.com/Articles/Read.aspx?GUID=8C1D2863-9FE5-43E9-BA8E-B21C2FFE5158/ (accessed April 14, 2009). In the symposium Paul Marshall, a Senior Fellow at Freedom House's Center for Religious Freedom, stated that persecution of Christians in the Islamic world is very widespread and that there are few Muslim countries where it does not occur. He also sees an upsurge of persecution in the Islamic world.

[23] For more details and the whole list see: http://www.opendoorsuk.org/resources/documents/WorldWatchList.pdf (accessed April 14, 2009).

[24] Patrick Poole, "Islam's Global War Against Christianity," *American Thinker*, http://www.americanthinker.com/2007/07/islams_global_war_against_chri.htmt. (accessed April 14, 2009). Poole writes that "the global war on Christianity by Islam is so massive in size and scope that it is virtually impossible to describe without trivializing it." The website Answering-Islam makes reference to this article.

[25] http://www.persecution.com (the website of the Voice of the Martyrs) reports the story of the martyrdom of Fatima Al-Mutairi. In August this year, a Muslim cleric and member of Saudi Arabia's Commission of the Promotion of Virtue and Prevention of Vice, killed his 26-year-old sister, Fatima Al-Mutairi, after she proclaimed her faith to her family, in the Eastern Province of Saudi Arabia. They also report about a Saudi member of the religious police cut his daughter's tongue off and burned her to death for converting to Christianity. The father, who works for the Commission for Promotion of Virtue and Prevention of Vice, killed his daughter following a debate on religion.

Doors[26] and the Voice of The Martyrs,[27] which encourages the global church to stand by their persecuted brothers and sisters. As a result even though they have not personally experienced the dark side of Islam, they identify with those who have and this information often colors the way they look at Islam in their own context. This attitude among Christians in the global church probably explains why the majority (55 percent) of the respondents to the questionnaire I conducted believe that the growth of the number of Muslims in Europe is dangerous for the freedom of Christians.[28]

History of Islam

Other Christians point out that Islam is spread by the sword;[29] it invaded Europe in the seventh century, expanded into the heartlands of Christianity, leading to the Crusades in the thirteenth and fourteenth centuries. Others point to the military campaigns of the Ottoman Empire in the fifteenth century, leading to various degrees of Islamization in their conquered Eastern European regions. Serbian Orthodox professor Trifkovic writes that "Islam is and always has been a religion of intolerance, a jihad without an end. Despite the way the apologists would like to depict it, Islam was spread by the sword and has been maintained by the sword throughout its history."[30] Others refer to the fact that in the heartland of Christianity (e.g. Algeria and Tunisia) after Islam arrived

[26] The website of Open Doors is: http://sb.od.org/

[27] The website of the Voice of the Martyrs is: http://www.persecution.com

[28] For more information, see chapter 5 and Appendix D.

[29] Mark Hartwig, "Spread By the Sword," *Answering Islam.org*, http://www.answering-islam.org/Terrorism/by_the_sword.html. (accessed April 14, 2009). In this article Hartwig examines the meaning of the word *jihad* in the Qur'an and the history of Islam, he concludes that the allegiance that Islam was spread by the sword is a fair charge, because "modernist interpretations notwithstanding, it is clear that military jihad—even in its expansionist form—is an authentic part of Islam."

[30] Serge Trifkovic, *The Sword of the Prophet: Islam, history, theology, impact on the world* (Boston: Regina Orthodox Press Inc, 2002),132.

on the scene, the church that previously blossomed was persecuted and gradually disappeared. Patrick Sookhdeo, Director of Barnabas Fund, a charity which assists persecuted Christians particularly in the Muslim World, points out that "sections of the church (e. g. North Africa) have disappeared completely in the face of the challenge of Islam."[31]

The Qur'an

Some Christians say that the real problem is not the Muslims themselves but the use of violence associated with them which goes back to the very heart and origin of Islam, namely to the *Qur'an* and the example of Muhammad.[32] In an article *Islam and Violence* placed on the website *answering-islam.org* an unknown author refers to 20 verses in the *Qur'an* that can and have been used in the history of Islam in support of violence in the name of God and the glories of martyrdom in a holy war and concludes that "a simple reading of such Qur'anic passages makes it obvious how easy it is for many Muslims to feel hatred and enmity against Jews, Christians and other non-Muslims." The article also points out that violence in Islam, whether in the form of terrorism, or the persecution of Christians or capital punishment for an individual who turns away from Islam or death threats on those who insult the prophet Muhammad, are not simply some isolated incidents or aberrations from the true and peaceful religion of Islam, but "goes to

[31] Patrick Sookhdeo, *Islam: the Challenge to the Church* (Wiltshire,UK: Isaac Publishing, 2006), 2.

[32] Trifkovic, 301. Trifkovic believes that the violent message of the Quran is a huge problem for all Muslims. "Islam, in Muhammad's texts and its codification, discriminates against us. It is extremely offensive. Those who submit to that faith must solve the problem they set themselves. Islam discriminates against all 'unbelievers.' Until the petrodollars support a Kuranic revisionism that does not, we should go for it with whips and scorpions, hammer and tongs. Secularists and believers of all other faiths must act together before it is too late."

the very roots of Islam as found in the Qur'an and the actions and teachings of the prophet of Islam himself."[33]

Almost a third of the respondents (31 percent) of the questionnaire I sent out believe that the Qur'an encourages terrorism, almost half (47 percent) believe it encourages violence against Christians, and 43 percent stated that because Muhammad was a warlord, fighting is part of what Islam is.[34]

The Ambition of Muslims: Islamization of Europe

Some Christians make reference to the fact that Islam is a missionary religion that trains and sends out missionaries around the world to promote Islam, which is called *dawah*.[35] Others believe that Muslims have a master plan to take over our countries and take possession of our neighborhoods, schools, and governments. Under the heading "The third conquest of Europe", Trifkovic gives many examples of how European Muslims are imposing their religion on Europe. He thinks that Muslim purposefully have large families, because

> most Muslim countries regard demography as a political weapon, they will gladly export their surplus population to Europe and Amer-

[33] Answering Islam. "Islam and Violence." http://www.answering-islam.org/Terrorism/islam_and_violence.html (accessed April 14,2009). Another article *Violence in the Bible and the Qur'an: A Christian perspective* on the same website comes to the same conclusion http://www.answering-islam.org/Terrorism/violence.html

[34] For more information, see chapter 5 and appendix D.

[35] In session 2 of the *course Engaging with Islam*, which is developed to train Christians to relate to Muslims, author Steve Green, says that the goal of the *Qur'an* is the movement from a minority group to the formation of an Islamic state, and that the goal of the devout Islamic community is to bring about an Islamic state, where *Shariah* law is enforced and brought about and where Muslims can live under the laws of Allah. Session 5 is devoted to the explanation of the Islamic concept of *dawah*. Green gives several examples of how Muslims do *dawah* in the West, namely through Islamic awareness weeks, book tables, television programs, through their participation in politics, in which Muslim politicians bring about Islamic laws, through banking, and through businesses. Samuel Green, *Engaging With Islam: A Training Course for Christians* (Kingsford, Australia: Australian Fellowship of Evangelical Students, 2006).

ica, aware that the bigger the diaspora, the greater the political influence it will exert, and the more concessions the Islamic world will be able to extort from the West... Islamic religious instruction in the newly planted Muslim communities on both sides of the Atlantic has been carried out by immigrant imams who have a clear agenda aimed at inculcating their Western-born wards with disdain and even hatred for their surroundings.[36]

According to the Christian website *Answering-Islam.org*, "the central goal of Islam is to establish Islamic law in every country, and this is the declared purpose of many Islamic organizations also in the USA and in Europe."[37] David Pawson, a prominent contemporary Bible teacher based in Great Britain, writer of more than thirty books, many of which have been translated in other languages, and a worldwide speaker, believes that he has received a prophetic revelation from God that Islam will take over England.[38]

As I have shown in the last chapter, other Christians point out that Europe is gradually becoming *Eurabia*, a continent that submits to the demands of Muslims.[39]

[36] Trifkovic, 283.

[37] Answering Islam. "Being a non-Muslim under Islamic rule." Answering Islam Home page. http://www.answering-islam.org/NonMuslims/index.htm (accessed April 14, 2009).

[38] David Pawson, *The Challenge of Islam to Christians* (London: Hodder & Stoughton, 2003).

In this book he writes: "While listening to a talk of Patrick Sookhdeo in 2002, I was suddenly overwhelmed with what could be described as a premonition that Islam will take over this country." (7) He also quotes a remark made at the opening of a mosque in Stockholm: "In the next fifty years we will capture the Western world for Islam. We have the men to do it; we have the money to do it; and, above all, we are already doing it." (21) He points to the growth of Islam in Britain and writes that education is being infiltrated (31) "Muslim leaders in Britain have been quite frank about their hopes of taking the United Kingdom for Allah and bringing not only Muslims but all of us under his laws (Shariah). To quote one: That must be our goal or we have no business here and may Allah give us success." (33).

[39] See footnote 23 of chapter one of this dissertation for more details.

Islam's Aggression is Against Israel

The Arab-Israeli conflict also influences the way Christians in Europe look at Islam. In a questionnaire I conducted, 70 percent of the respondents agreed with or were not willing to explicitly disagree with the statement that "it is because of Islam, there are troubles in Israel."[40] Many Christians, especially evangelicals, back the State of Israel, claiming that its establishment in 1948 fulfils biblical prophecies.[41] Many Christians believe the Christian community should oppose those who hate Israel, which of course are Muslims. In March 2004, four major international Christian pro-Israel organizations with activities in Europe launched *The European Coalition for Israel* to address the issue of growing anti-Semitism and anti-Zionism in Europe. During their 4th Annual Policy Conference in September 2006, attended by 100 participants from 17 different nations, several speakers pointed out that the same forces which are trying to wipe Israel off the map would also want to conquer Europe and that the same militant Islamic forces which are waging a war against Israel would also like to see Europe conquered.[42]

[40] For more information, see chapter 5 and appendix D.

[41] Steve Bell, *Grace for Muslims?* (Milton Keynes, UK: Authentic Media, 2006), 52. In this book Bell writes" One reason of the negative attitude of many Christians towards Muslims is the over-romanticing of the Holy Land that has come about through the idealized teaching of biblical history and biblical prophecy." (52). Also Chawkat Moucarry in his book *Faith to Faith* in which he examines the claims of Christianity and Islam, considers this an important issue in the Christian-Muslim relations. Moucarry Chawkat, *Faith to Faith: Christianity & Islam in dialogue* (Nottingham: Intervarsity Press, 2001).

[42] European Coalition for Israel, "4th Annual Policy Conference: Promoting The Reform Process In The Middle East -what Role Can The European Union Play?," *European Coalition For Israel*, September, 2006, http://www.ec4i.org/content/blogsection/6/49// (accessed April 1, 2009).

Muslims' Unresponsiveness to the Gospel

Other Christians indicate that they fear Muslims because of the fact that for centuries Muslims have been among the most unresponsive people to the Gospel of Jesus Christ. In addition Muslims are very outspoken against some of the main Christian doctrines such as the divinity of Christ and his crucifixion. Also, it is noted that even many Europeans, who were brought up as Christians, are becoming Muslims.[43]

Consequences of Islamophobia

For the average European, Islam's progress in establishing itself as a permanent feature of European culture has been and continues to be a difficult phenomenon to accept. For many decades, Muslims were exclusively perceived as temporary guests relegated to the fringes of society. Their evolution—from foreigner to permanent resident to citizen—has been troubling. European societies essentially have a negative response to the growing visibility of Islam in their midst.[44]

Among the consequences of the negative perception of Islam in Europe, there are two worth discussing here: 1) marginalization and discrimination; 2) xenophobia and the resurgence of nationalism.

[43] During the break of a church meeting in Slowakia in 2003, after I shared about the importance of reaching out to Muslims with the love of Christ, one of the people present, handed me a piece of paper on which he had written the Bible verse Matthew 7:6 "Do not give dogs what is sacred, do not throw your pearls to pigs. If you do, they may trample them under their feet, and then turn and tear you to pieces."

[44] Pauly believes that this results from "widespread Western misperceptions of Islam as a monolithic faith whose adherents possess a universal penchant for the proliferation of radical religious fundamentalism." Pauly, 2.

Cesari states that "Islam is systematically conflated with threats to international or domestic order." Jocelyne Cesari, "Mosque Conflicts in Europe," *Journal of Ethnic and Migrations Studies*, Special Issue., (November 2005), 2.

Marginalization, Discrimination, and Exclusion

Directly or indirectly linked to the predominantly negative perception of Islam in Europe is the fact that many Muslims in Europe experience marginalization and social discrimination or exclusion. Sometimes this exclusion is self-inflicted (e. g. due to reluctance to learn the local language, unwillingness to attend or finish education, a negative view of Western society resulting in a withdrawal from it). The socio-economic situation for many Muslims in Europe is far from good. In every country in Europe, the rate of Muslim unemployment is higher than that among European nationals.[45] Muslim's level of income is lower than the European average. Muslims tend to live in overcrowded and under-serviced apartment buildings in crime-ridden urban areas.[46]

Muslim immigrants often encounter multiple forms of discrimination when applying for housing in more coveted areas, or when looking for jobs or places of internship, they are refused entry into bars and night clubs and are treated with hostility because of their appearances. Muslims are often profiled and harassed by law enforcement agents who randomly demand to see their identification papers, though they have committed no crime.[47] Many Muslim immigrants in Europe are excluded from the economic, political, and social benefits afforded to the majority populations. In a study, based on in-depth interviews, conducted between August 2005

[45] Cesari, *Islam and Democracy*, 22.

[46] Ibid., 23.

[47] Trica Danielle Keaton, who interviewed fourteen Muslim girls, between fifteen and nineteen years old, in Paris, points out that the youth of Arab and African descent in Paris suffer humiliation at the hands of the authorities and their civil and citizenship rights are continually violated by people who treat them as foreigners simply on the basis of the color of their skin and they are both assimilated culturally and excluded socially. She points out that many young Muslims in Europe suffer from racialized discriminations, which manifests itself in the most basic social structures, including employment, housing, education, social services, the criminal justice system, and the relations with the police. Trica Danielle Keaton, *Muslim Girls and the Other France: Race, Identity Politics & Social Exclusion* (Bloomington: Indiana University Press, 2006), x.

and January 2006, with members of Muslim communities in ten EU member states, the European Monitoring Centre on Racism and Xenophobia (EUMC) concluded that migrants throughout Europe experience discriminatory practices to a significant extent, particularly with regard to employment and in the sphere of commercial transactions. Nearly one third of respondents stated that they experienced discrimination through being refused access to jobs, missing promotions, or being harassed at work. More than one in four respondents claimed to have experienced discrimination in commercial transactions, either through denial of access to housing, or credit or loans. In the opinion of the interviewees, many Muslims in the European Union feel excluded from economic, social and cultural life. According to the interviewees, even when Muslims are citizens of a Member State, they can still feel a sense of exclusion. They feel that they are perceived as "foreigners" who are a threat to society, and treated with suspicion. This feeling is reported to be stronger among young European born Muslims than their parents. While the second and third generations are in many ways more integrated than the first, at the same time their expectations are greater and so the consequent exclusion is more keenly felt.[48]

Xenophobia and Resurgence of Nationalism

In every European country that is home to Muslims issues of race have reemerged.[49] Matters involving race, religion, and ethnicity are all put together. The influx of Muslim immigrants into Europe coincided with the growth of far-right political parties. Cesari believes that the most important reason why the parties of the Extreme Right seem to have gained a firm foothold in European

[48] The European Monitoring Centre on Racism and Xenophobia (EUMC)."Perceptions of discrimination and Islamophobia". http://fra.europa.eu/fraWebsite/attachments/Perceptions_EN.pdf (accessed April 14,2009).

[49] Cesari, *Islam and Democracy*, 29.

political life is "the ability of these movements to present Islam as an unyielding force, incapable of being assimilated into the national culture, by emphasizing both the fragility and the importance of European cultural values."[50] Unfortunately, Christians sometimes seem to sympathize with the ideas of the extreme right. A questionnaire circulated by the author shows that 60 percent of the respondents agree with the way Geert Wilders, a Dutch MP and head of an extreme right party, perceives Islam.[51]

Analyzing Fear

Most of the facts that are used to justify one's fear of Islam and Muslims contain elements of truth. Terrorism in the name of Islam exists. There are Muslims that seek to overthrow governments in the West in order to establish a Muslim state. There are intolerant verses in the *Qur'an*. Christians are being persecuted in many Islamic countries. There is no point in denying these facts. Of course, one could counter each argument with other arguments by pointing to how Muslim scholars interpret the violent verses of the Qur'an in a less strict way as would seem clear to the casual reader.[52] Or one could point out that Muslim extremists make up a tiny percentage of all Muslims. One could also take another approach

[50] Cesari, *Islam and Democracy*, 31. She also writes that "Although most of these political parties had already been present, their popularity grew once they linked the issues of the need to defend national identity and the recent increase in Muslim immigration."

[51] For more information, see chapter 5 and Appendix D.

[52] Two key verses that are important in the discussion on the peaceful or aggressive nature of Islam, are Sura 9:5: "*When the sacred months are past, then slay the polytheists, wherever you find them and take them and besiege them*" and Sura 9:29: "*Fight the idolators until they pay the jizya (poll tax) from their wealth submissively*" *(Sura 9:29)* The first one is called 'the sword verse'; Sura 9:29 is often referred to as "the jizya verse", but occasionally also as the sword verse. Many Muslim scholars have written about Sura 9:5 and Sura 9:29 and the verses are interpreted differently, as pointed out by Jane Dammen McAuliffe in *Encyclopaedia of the Qur'an* Brill, London Boston, 2006), Section Expeditions and Battles, 151: "... early Muslim exegetes preferred to interpret the sword verse in its context, that is, in relation to the situation of the Prophet when it was

by showing that Christianity has a violent past, and that the Bible too contains intolerant verses, or that Israel is not only a victim but also a perpetrator of violence.[53]

Of course, there is justification to fear violence that takes place in the name of Islam. Not all fear is wrong. Nevertheless, it is important to realize that fear is based on perception. Or more precisely, fear is caused by one's perception of reality. Some perceptions might be accurate, but one also needs to be willing to recognize that perceptions could be distortion of the reality. As has been argued above, *Islamophobia* is often based on a distorted perception of the reality.

When one looks beneath the attitude of fear, one might discover that it probably has more to do with oneself and one's fallen human nature than with the words or deeds of others. As a result of sin, humanity seems to approach the "unknown other" with a negative attitude and with suspicion instead of giving that "unknown other" the benefit of the doubt. The attitude that was already evident after the Fall in the relationship between Adam and Eve, has become part of every human being on the face of the earth. This same attitude seems to lay at the foundation of the fear of Islam and Muslims among Christians.

revealed and in association with the verses surrounding it. Q 9:1–5 are believed to have been revealed on the eve of the raid on Tabuk, when many of the pagans and hypocrites who had treaty obligations with the Prophet resisted joining him on the battlefield. Though al-Suddi explains the verses as a repudiation of Muhammad's agreement with all pagans, al-Tabart, al-Zamakhshari, and others, deny that the Qur'an could decree such intolerance. They divide Mohammad's non-monotheist allies into offensive and inoffensive groups and insist that the repudiation applied only to those non-monotheists who had violated their agreements." Jane Dammen McAuliffe, ed., *Encyclopaedia of the*

[53] The subject of war and judgment in Scriptures is beyond the scope of this dissertation, but it is a topic Christians need to look at and understand, as it will come up over and over again in dealing with Muslims.

Fear: Result of the Sinful Nature

Dr. Paul Weller, of the University of Derby, who researched *Islamophobia* and religious discrimination in Britain, historically and contemporarily, links *Islamophobia* to what he calls "the nasty side of human nature."[54] In biblical terms, one would say, the sinful human nature.

In discussing in which way the effects of this nasty side of human nature can be dealt with, Weller refers to the book *Moving Beyond Sectarianism: Religion, Conflict and Reconciliation in Northern Ireland*, by Joseph Liechty and Cecelia Clegg. In this book, the authors look at the way in which people in Ireland, including Christians, developed, cultivated and tried to overcome a hatred for "the other." The authors speak of the phenomenon of sectarianism, and characterize such an approach to the other as:

> A system of attitudes, actions, beliefs and structures at personal, communal and institutional levels which always involves religion, and typically involves a negative mixing of religion and politics
>
> which arises as a distorted expression of positive, human needs especially for belonging, identity, and the free expression of difference
>
> and is expressed in destructive patterns of relating:
> hardening the boundaries between groups
> overlooking others
> belittling, dehumanizing, or demonizing others
> justifying or collaborating in the domination of others
> physically or verbally intimidating or attacking others.

Liechty and Clegg developed a scale of sectarian danger consisting of eleven points all representing approaches to marking or evaluating difference:

> We are different, we behave differently
> We are right
> We are right and you are wrong

[54] Dr. Paul Weller, "Addressing Religious Discrimination and Islamophobia: Muslims and Liberal Democracies, the case of the United Kingdom," *Journal of Islamic Studies* 17, no. 3 (2006), 295–325.

You are a less adequate version of what we are
You are not what you say you are
We are in fact what you say you are
What you are doing is evil
You are so wrong that you forfeit ordinary rights
You are less than human
You are evil
You are demonic.[55]

Fear and Our Identity

This scale brings out something that might be considered a key element when looking at fear of Islam, namely the will for identity or the fear to lose one's identity. Robert Purkiss, Management Board Chairman of the European Monitoring Centre for Racism and Xenophobia (EUMC) believes that the conceptions of European identity are probably among the strongest drivers of *Islamophobia.*

> Despite Islam's contribution to the development of European societies, it has been excised from the prevailing understanding of Europe's identity as Christian and white. Islam has longed served as Europe's "other", as a symbol for a distinct culture, religion and even ethnicity that characterizes non-Europeans.[56]

[55] Joseph Liechty and Cecelia Clegg, *Moving Beyond Sectarianism: Religion, Conflict and Reconciliation in Northern Ireland* (Dublin: The Colomba Press, 2001), 245.

[56] European Union Agency for Fundamental Rights."The fight against Anti-Semitism and Islamophobia: Bringing Communities Together." FRA. http://fra.europa.eu/fraWebsite/products/publications_reports/thematic_reports/pub_tr_fight_antisemitism_islamophobia_03_en.htm (accessed April 14, 2009).

Matti Bunzl, "Between anti-Semitism and Islamophobia: Some thoughts on the new Europe," *American Ethnologist* 32, no. 4 (2005) 499–508. In this article, Bunzl, of the University of Illinois at Urbana—Champaign states that "at the heart of the Islamophobic discourse is the question of civilization, the notion that Islam engenders a worldview that is fundamentally incompatible with and inferior to Western culture."

Tariq Modood believes there is an anti-Muslim wind blowing across the European continent, based on the perception "that Muslims are making politically exceptional, culturally unreasonable or theologically alien demands upon European' states." Tariq Modood, "Muslims and the Politics of Difference," *Political Quarterly* 74, no. 1 (2003): 100.

Europe is afraid to lose its identity with the influx of Muslims.[57] Claims that Islam is totally different and "other" often involves stereotypes and claims about us (non-Muslims) as well as about them (Muslims), and the notion that Europeans (non-Muslims) are superior. Europeans are civilized, reasonable, generous, efficient, sophisticated, enlightened, and non-sexist. They (Muslims) are primitive, violent, irrational, scheming, disorganized, and oppressive.

The presence of Islam in Europe seems to coincide with the identity crisis Christianity in Europe faces. As a result of secularization, Christianity in Europe has lost most of its former power and influence. The decline of Christianity in Europe coincides with the growing number of religious Muslims in Europe. As a result, church buildings that were no longer used because the congregations had died out are turned into mosques. At first glance this development gives the impression that Islam is gradually replacing Christianity in Europe as the main religion. Because of this development, Christians are encouraged to defend Europe's Western and Christian roots.[58]

The presence of many Muslims in Europe forces Christians to deal with the issue of identity and diversity.[59] The pluralism of Eu-

[57] Just over a quarter (26 percent) of the respondents to the questionnaire I conducted agreed or strongly agreed with the statement that Islam is the biggest threat to our national identity. Of these 83 percent were African immigrants in the Netherlands. For more information, see chapter 5 and Appendix D.

[58] Serge Trifkovic believes that "like communism, Islam relies on a domestic fifth column—the Allah-worshiping Rosenbergs, Philbys, Blunts and Hisses—to subvert the civilized world." To combat this, he suggests that Europe should defend its Western and Christian roots. "Those roots much be defended, in the full knowledge that those who subscribe to Islam and its civilization are aliens, regardless of their clothes, their professions or their places of residence." Trifkovic, The Sword of the prophet, 292

[59] The Kroatian theologian MiroslavVolf believes it may not be too much to claim that the future of our world will depend on how we deal with identity and difference. "The issue is urgent. The ghettos and battlefields throughout the world—in the living rooms, the inner cities, or on the mountain ranges—testify indisputably to its importance." Miroslav Volf, *Exclusion and Embrace* (Nashville, US: Abingdon Press, 1996), 20.

ropean societies seems to inflame exclusivisms and highlight ethnocentricity among Christians.[60] Perhaps one's fear of Islam is a fear of losing one's identity, which leads to an attitude of exclusion.

Fear of Islam and the Sin of Exclusion

As shown earlier in this chapter, *Islamophobia* in Europe results in Muslims being frequently excluded from the economic, social, and cultural life of the nation. The exclusion that Muslims in Europe experience has several dimensions: being ignored, overlooked, or not given service in a shop or restaurant, having their ideas or opinions being devalued or ignored, being avoided or having others physically move away, being excluded from conversation or activities, being excluded from the right of citizenship, being excluded from certain jobs or promotions, or from renting apartments, from living in certain sections of the city etc.[61]

One should be careful not to hide behind structures, communities, or leaders, and ignore making exclusion a personal matter. One must acknowledge that not only does society exclude Muslims, but Christians who fear Islam and Muslims are guilty of excluding the Muslim from their hearts, their love, their compassion, their concern, their interest, and their lives.

The Croatian theologian Miroslav Volf, in his book *Exclusion and Embrace*, looks in a theological way at ethnic and cultural conflicts, involving attitudes of exclusion directed at others, particularly against the background of the inter-ethnic problems in the

[60] Musk wonders "Is it the necessity of relating to one another that highlights the inbred ethnocentredness of us all? We didn't know we couldn't get on together until it became plain we had to." Bill Musk, *Holy War, Why do some Muslims become fundamentalists?* (London: Monarch Books, 2003), 259.

[61] For specific examples see the EUMC report "Perceptions of discrimination and Islamophobia", particularly pages 23, 28, 39, 42, 59. http://fra.europa.eu/fraWebsite/attachments/Perceptions_EN.pdf
(accessed April 14,2009).

Balkans. Volf believes that exclusion names "what permeates a good many of sins we commit against our neighbors."[62] It is this sin of exclusion that causes Europeans to react out of fear and anger to all those who are not within its circle. Fear of Muslims and Islam often grows out of an attitude of exclusion.

Volf gives the following four characteristics of an attitude and a culture of exclusion. First, exclusion, making the other an enemy that must be pushed away and driven out of one's space; second, exclusion considers the other as a nonentity that can be disregarded and abandoned; third, exclusion fails to recognize the other as someone who in his or her otherness belongs to the community of humankind; and fourth, exclusion considers the other an inferior being who must either be assimilated or be subjugated.[63]

Such a culture of exclusion often characterizes the relationship between the West and Islam or Muslims. As pointed out earlier, the attitude of Christians hardly differs from that of their secular countrymen. Because Christians often find it difficult to distance themselves from their culture, they echo its reigning opinions and mimic its practices, including those of *Islamophobia.* Mennonite author, teacher and missionary, Gordon D. Nickel, writes that Christians cannot follow national feelings as their approach toward Muslims.

> If it indeed happens that a Muslim nation becomes a political enemy of our own country, then the command of Jesus becomes our rule, "Love your enemies, do good to those who hate you, bless those who curse you, pray for those who mistreat you." (Luke 6:27, 28)... The mission of God to save a lost world—including Muslims—simply takes precedence over national goals of defense or domination.[64]

Christians have to understand that, like Jews and Muslims, they can never be first of all Asians or Americans, British or Dutch, and

[62] Volf, 72.

[63] Volf, 67.

[64] Gordon D. Nickel, *Peaceable Witness among Muslims* (Ontario, Canada: Herald Press, 1999), 22.

then Christians.[65] Instead of being molded by their way of thinking, Christians need to be agents of change and transformation in our societies (Rom. 12:1, 2).[66] In order to be agents of change and transformation, Christians need to be transformed themselves and develop another attitude towards Islam and Muslims.

Developing Another Culture, Another Attitude and Another Behavior Towards Islam and Muslims

The Christian's thinking, attitude, and behavior with regard to Muslims, and even militant Muslims, should be guided by God's self-giving love manifested at the cross of Golgotha. Volf points out that: "As God does not abandon the godless to their evil but gives the divine self for them in order to receive them into divine communion through atonement, so also should we, whoever our enemies and whoever we may be."[67]

When a follower of Jesus Christ considers his or her attitude towards others, including Muslims, in the light of the self-giving love of God, it becomes clear that negative attitudes of fear, prejudice and suspicion, which are part of a culture of exclusion, are inappropriate, and should be replaced by (1) another culture, namely a culture of embrace; (2) another attitude, namely a grace-response and (3) another behavior, namely one that is based on the model of the cross.

[65] "At the very core of Christian identity lies an all-encompassing change of loyalty from a given culture with its gods to the God of all cultures." Volf, 40.

[66] Volf refers to an empirical research conducted by Ralph Premdas in a number of countries, which has shown that "the inter-communal antipathies present in the society at large are reflected in the attitudes of churches and their adherents." Volf, 36, 37.

[67] Volf, 23.

A Culture of Embrace

The attitude of fear, prejudice, and suspicion that characterizes many Christians in Europe towards Muslims and Islam belongs to a culture of exclusion. The desired attitude on the basis of the self-giving love of God is motivated by grace and, to use Volf's metaphor, is part of a culture of embrace.

> The work of reconciliation should proceed under the assumption that, though the behavior of a person may be judged as deplorable, even demonic, no one should ever be excluded from the will to embrace, because at the deepest level, the relationship to others does not rest on their moral performance and therefore cannot be undone by the lack of it... At the core of the Christian faith lies the persuasion that the others need not be perceived as innocent in order to be loved, but ought to be embraced even when they are perceived as wrongdoers. The story of the cross is about God who desires to embrace precisely the "sons and daughters" of hell.[68]

Volf uses this metaphor of embrace to express "the absolute indiscriminate and strictly immutable will to give ourselves to others and welcome them, to readjust our identities to make space for them."[69] Such willingness to embrace someone who is perceived as unworthy, a possible enemy and guilty is possible in the biblical sense only when the Holy Spirit works in us and enables us to resist the power of exclusion. Volf gives four features of a culture and attitude of embrace: (1) repentance; (2) forgiveness; (3) making space for the other; (4) a willingness to forget or overlook the evil suffered.[70]

Repentance

Those who fear Islam and Muslims justify their attitude by pointing to the other, the "them" who are so aggressive, intolerant etc., but genuine repentance demands that one refuses "to explain

[68] Volf, 85.

[69] Volf, 29.

[70] Volf, chapter III (99–165).

our behavior and accuse others, and simply take our wrongdoing upon ourselves."[71] Islamophobes need to repent of *Islamophobia*[72] in order to develop a genuine relationship with Muslims.[73]

Forgiveness

A second characteristic of the culture of embrace is forgiveness. According to Volf, "Forgiveness is the boundary between exclusion and embrace. It heals the wounds that the power-acts of exclusion have inflicted and breaks down the dividing wall of hostility."[74] Forgiveness is the only way to break the cycle of vengeance.

The Psalms make clear how Christians are able to satisfy their thirst for justice and calm their passion for revenge so as to practice forgiveness, namely bringing the puzzlement and rage over injustice into the presence of the God of justice.[75] Reflecting on these Psalms could help a Christian to overcome their attitude of fear and exclusion towards Muslims.

Making Space for the Other

A third aspect of the culture of embrace, according to Volf, is "making space for the other," making peace, restoring the broken

71 Volf, 119.

72 An example of a collective repentance on the part of the Christians of their wrong attitudes can be found in the "Declaration on Christian Attitudes Towards Muslims", drafted by the Association of International Missions Services (AIMS) in cooperation with AIMS member agencies focusing on the Islamic world. This declaration was published in the International Journal of Frontier Missions, 13, no (July-September 1996 and can be read on their website http://www.ijfm.org/PDFs_IJFM/13_3_PDFs/02_Declar_on_Musli.pdf (accessed April 14, 2009). A slightly adopted version of this declaration is found in lesson 9 of the course *Encountering the World of Islam*, which will be discussed in the next chapter.

73 Musk acknowledges that also Christians need to walk a path of repentance. "It is time for us to recognize issues of injustice, many of which inflame various fundamentalisms, and speak out against them per se, in defence of whoever is being victimized." Musk, *Holy War*, 267.

74 Volf, 125.

75 E.g. Psalm 12, 44, 58, 83, 109, 137, 139.

communion. God has made space for us and therefore such attitude should be the mark of a Christian. Volf points out that: "At the heart of the cross is Christ's stance of not letting the other remain an enemy and of creating space in himself for the offender to come in."[76] Having been embraced by God, "we must make space for others in ourselves and invite them in—even our enemies."[77]

Forgetting, or Overlooking, the Evil Suffered

The fourth characteristic of a culture of embrace is the willingness to forget or to overlook the evil suffered, the insult received, the maltreatment, the prejudices, the stereotypes used to exclude you. In this instance we are called to follow God's example:

> God forgets humanity's sins in the same way God forgives humanity's sins: by taking sins away from humanity and placing them upon God-self. How will human beings be able to forget the horrors of history? Because at the center of the new world that will emerge after "the first things have passed away" there will stand a throne, and on the throne there will sit the Lamb who has "taken away the sin of the world" and erased their memory (Rev. 22:1–4; John 1:29).[78]

A Grace Response Towards Muslims

The example of God's self-giving love as manifested on the cross of Christ should encourage Christians to approach Muslims with a willingness to embrace them. The metaphor of embrace, which Volf uses, could be theologically defined as "grace". In other words: a "willingness to embrace," could also be defined as a "grace response."

In his book *Grace for Muslims?* Mission leader Steve Bell defines "grace-response" as follows:

[76] Volf., 126.
[77] Ibid., 129.
[78] Ibid., 140.

> A grace-response is a willingness to alter the default mechanism in our brains which causes us to fear the unfamiliar in another person; being prepared to give others the benefit of the doubt and make an effort to find out why they behave as they do. A grace response is willing to include the other person within the scope of God's love and the Great Commission of Jesus Christ, rather than imagining there is an exclusion clause which puts them beyond our concern.[79]

I would like to argue that an attitude of grace, on the part of Christians with regard to Muslims in Europe, consists of the following characteristics.

Dialogue

Dialogue is a key aspect to overcome the attitude of *Islamophobia,*[80] because it helps one to know the other better and it helps one to learn to see oneself as others see him or her. The word *dialogue* is used very broadly and often stirs up negative emotions among Evangelical Christians.[81] Nevertheless, dialogue is necessary between Christians and Muslims to overcome the animosity between them.[82]

[79] Steve Bell, *Grace for Muslims, the journey from fear to faith* (Milton Keynes, UK: Authentic Media, 2006), 1.

[80] Michael Ancram, "Clash or Dialogue of Civilisations?" (speech, Oxford Centre for Islamic Studies, May 16, 2003) Michael Ancram, http://www.michaelancram.com/sp_display.aspx?id=69 (accessed April 13, 2009). Ancram stated that a key to begin dialogue is to understand each other's fears, because fear is at the core of the animosity. Fear of being overwhelmed by the other. On one side fear of Islamization of Europe and on the other side fear of Westoxification of Muslims in Europe.

[81] Patrick Sookhdeo in his book *Islam: the Challenge to the Church*, writes that interfaith dialogue initiatives have some inherent risks which makes him reject such approach. Bat Ye'or, who is not an Evangelical Christian, considers Christian initiatives toward interfaith dialogue with Muslims as opening the door for the islamization of Christianity Bat Ye'or, *Eurabia: The Euro-Arab Axis*, 211.

[82] In her book *Muslims and Christians Face to Face* Kate Zebiri analyses modern Muslim writings on Christianity and Christian writings on Islam. In this book she refers to discursive dialogue: "In some respects, the position of mainstream Muslims is comparable to that of conservative evangelical Christians, who initially at least expressed strong reservations about dialogue, fearing that it would lead to religious syncretism and compromising the essentials of faith." Muslims concerned with *da'wah* and evangelical

When Christians look at Islam or Muslims, the temptation is to compare one's own ideals with the other's realities. In answering the question, "How should Christians respond to resurgent Islam and to fundamentalist Muslims?" author and theologian Dr. Bill Musk believes that:

> We must begin, in relating to fundamentalists as to others, by listening and learning to empathize; trying to discern what life is about from their perspective. We must be careful not to stereotype 'fundamentalists' for they are not all the same. Equally, we need to recognize that not all Muslims are Islamists.[83]

Related to this perception is the necessity to understand the Muslims' history and background. Ancram, Member of Parliament in the United Kingdom, points out that:

> An understanding of the past provides the background that is necessary to inform dialogue. It discloses the sources of the fears that in turn have given rise to the bitterness and the hatred. It rapidly becomes the basic building block of discourse. Knowing how and why the knots of hatred and mistrust came to be tied is the only route to loosen, to unravel, and eventually to undo them.[84]

Dialogue is one of the best ways that these underlying fears can be assuaged.

One gets a picture of the kind of dialogue that gets beneath the surface in Luke's description of Jesus in the temple at the age of twelve (Luke 2: 46, 47).[85] Such dialogue consists of (1) social interaction; (2) listening; (3) asking questions and (4) offering answers.[86]

Christians are likely to give priority to 'discursive dialogue; at the very least this may serve to eradicate distortions and misunderstandings and thereby eliminate obstacles to conversion."Kate Zebiri, *Muslims and Christians Face to Face*, 38.

[83] Musk, *Holy War*, 267.

[84] Michael Ancram, "Clash or Dialogue of Civilisations?" (speech, Oxford Centre for Islamic Studies, May 16, 2003).

[85] Colin Chapman, *Cross & Crescent: responding to the Challenge of Islam* (Downers Grove, IL, USA: IVP Books, 2007), 24.

[86] Ibid.

Speak Well of the Muslim Neighbor

Against the hate speeches or judgmental way of referring to Muslims, or stereotyping, Christians should be encouraged to speak well of our Muslim neighbors. The ninth of the Ten Commandments is "You shall not give false testimony against your neighbor" (Ex. 20:16). When applying this commandment to Muslim neighbors, it implies that when one speaks about Islam, one should seek to be as truthful as possible. Sometimes fear can lead people to exaggerate situations. Essentially, Islam is what a Muslim says it is.

Christians should be careful to interpret the Qur'an correctly and not take verses out of context, taking into consideration how these verses have been or are interpreted by Muslims scholars. Christians should be willing to listen to Muslims and to learn to see the world through their eyes and let them interpret their religion for us.[87]

Being Critical Without Being Judgmental

Volf states that to fight exclusion successfully, what is needed are "nonexclusionary judgments passed by persons willing to embrace the other."[88] Applying this suggestion to Islam, one could say that one does not have to embrace Islam, in order to embrace Muslims. One can pass judgment on Islam, without excluding Muslims. Volf acknowledges that:

> It is true that sometimes judgments lead to exclusion and can be an act of exclusion. But the remedy for exclusionary judgments are more adequate judgments based on a distinction between differentiation

[87] This is what Musk seeks to do in his book *Kissing Cousins: Christians and Muslims face to face*, in which he wants to help the readers "to look beyond the systematizing processes of institutionalized religion to search for the intentions of faith which allows us to let each faith be its own interpreter." Bill Musk, *Kissing Cousin? Christians and Muslims face to face* (Oxford: Monarch Books, 2005), 15.

[88] Volf, 65.

and exclusion and made with humility that counts with our proclivity to misperceive and misjudge because we desire to exclude.[89]

We should be able to respect Islam and Muslims, without agreeing with their teachings. Colin Chapman suggests a good middle way between demonizing Islam or Muslims and being naïve about the intentions of some of them, as follows:

> A middle way between these two extremes would mean (a) being realistic about the real intentions of *some* Muslims, (b) recognizing the diversity among Muslims and relating to them as individuals and groups with openness and honesty, (c) taking a firm stand on issues of human rights, (d) working for the common good of the whole society, (e) demonstrating a fundamental respect for Islam (without agreeing with all its teaching), and (f) unapologetically commending the Christian faith through word and deed.[90]

While acknowledging the injustices that have taken place in name of Christianity, one must at the same time speak out against injustices done in the name of Islam and also be ready to ask difficult questions of Muslim friends. Colin Chapman suggested that Christians be prepared for "hard talk" with Muslims and Islamists, and he lists some of the questions we may want to ask.[91]

There might also be times when, alongside Muslims, one would do well to join the struggle against common enemies. Islam's critique of the Western worldview should provoke Christians to stop and reflect. According to Musk:

> We are the sixth generation children of the Enlightenment and it is becoming increasingly plain that secularization is not the benign or neutral god our fathers believed it to be. Secularized society is but a posh name for "pagan society." We don't marry up to four wives, but

[89] Ibid., 68.

[90] Colin Chapman, "Christian Responses to Islam, Islamism and Islamic Terrorism," *Cambridge Papers* 16, no. 2 (June 2007).

[91] Ibid. For example: Are you prepared to be critical of your history? Do you accept the concept of universal human rights as they have developed in recent years? What about the means that you use to achieve your goals? Does the end justify the means? Are you willing to accept the existence of pluralist societies?

> we do engage in sequential polygamy. There is no religious favoritism in our secular societies, except that our TV programs, school textbooks, and public arts are loaded with references to the occult. We don't cut off hands for theft, but we casually kill our unborn in their millions . . .[92]

It is sometimes assumed that when religious and theological misunderstandings are cleared up, Muslims and Christians will automatically enjoy more cordial relations, but as Zebiri rightly points out, even when Muslims have a good grasp of Christianity:

> there is a good chance that a Muslim will still be genuinely repelled and even offended by it. One sometimes encounters a kind of aesthetic aversion to central Christian truths, particularly the Crucifixion. Muslim rejection of Christian beliefs cannot always be attributed to misunderstanding, obtuseness or polemicism. The same would have to be true of Christians who find it difficult to see in the Muhammad of history an ideal model of human conduct, or who have reservations about parts of the Qur'an. This is not necessarily as inauspicious for Muslim-Christian relations as it may seem; it may be existentially impossible wholly to suspend judgment in areas which directly impinge on one's own truth-claims, but as in life generally, one does not need to denigrate those with whom one disagrees.[93]

The Cross as a Model for a Relationship with Muslims

For Christians, the challenge is to draw back from seeing Muslims or Islam as "the enemy." Often Christians consider Islam a threat, have strong prejudices against Muslims, and find it easier to believe that extremists represents true Islam as opposed to moderates,[94] particularly pointing to the terrorism of Islamic extremists in the West and the persecution of Christians in predominantly Muslim countries.

[92] Musk, *Holy War*, 251.

[93] Zebiri, 234.

[94] Although in the questionnaire I conducted, 68 percent of the respondents did not believe that Muslim extremists (e. g. Taliban, Al Quaida) represent true Islam.

In response to these facts, I could point to moderate Muslims, to Muslims who interpret the Qur'an in an more peaceful way, to Muslims who are working day and night to build social cohesion in their cities, to Muslim Background believers who are accepted and respected by their family members, and to Muslims who truly are committed to seeking the welfare of Europe and its citizens and values, etc.

But such arguments and counter arguments seems to point to the fact that if Muslims were more loveable, Europeans could love them; if they were more trustworthy, they would trust them; if they were less aggressive, they would not fear them; if Muslims were more peaceful, they would leave them in peace. But this kind of reasoning violates the principle of grace found in the Bible, and the example of embracing of enemies and creating space within oneself for them.

Musk points out that,

> even where some Muslims cast themselves as opponents of (in their view) "unbelieving" Christians and Jews, and make Westerners their enemies, the words of Christ about our attitude towards 'enemies' needs to color our responses. The kingdom of God grows in peoples' hearts, not via the sword, but via the Cross.[95]

For Muhammad, the use of weaponry to achieve God's goal was permitted and commanded. As a result of the Qur'anic command to use force to achieve supremacy, Muslims speak about the nature of *jihad*. Nevertheless, Musk asserts:

> for Jesus, such approach to the appropriation of physical force was an option he consistently refused to take. In Islam, the progression from preacher to powerful ruler was legitimized by God himself... In Christianity, the call is continually for Christians to have that mind in them that was in Christ Jesus—to walk the way of humility and vulnerability.[96]

[95] Musk, *Holy War*, 10, 267.

[96] Musk, *Kissing Cousins*, 218.

But instead of love and humility, many Christians live by and express an attitude of fear. Such attitude comes out particularly when someone says one should not be afraid of Muslims or Islam.

Gordon Showell-Rogers, General Secretary of the European Evangelical Alliance, during the Alliance's General Assembly in October 2007, said that Christians have nothing at all to fear from any form of Islam. Several people disagreed with Showell-Rogers strongly and said he lost his mind.[97]

In order for Europe to become free of *Islamophobia* and related issues, what is needed are not only new laws against religious racism, less discrimination, a more balanced representation of Muslims in the media, an equal access of Muslims to education and the workforce, and a society where people of all races and religions live harmoniously together. The primary need is for people, transformed people, who want to be instruments of transformation and who are able to live in harmony with others, including those that could be enemies. Volf states that "What is needed are social agents that are shaped by the values of God's kingdom and therefore capable of participating in the project of authentic social transformation."[98]

I believe that such transformational, social agents have three defining characteristics: (1) they live their lives in the light of the cross; (2) they share the Gospel in the way of the cross; and (3) they are willing to bear the scandal of the cross.

[97] Gordon Showell-Rogers, "Christians have nothing to fear of Islam," speech delivered to General Assembly European Evangelical Alliance, October 17, 2007, Greece. In response to the article of this speech, someone wrote: "I think we have A LOT to be concerned with concerning Islam. Since ISAAC is the Son of the Promise and there is no other answer to the Ishmaelites than that. To try in any way to embrace Islam as a 'brother' descended from Abraham, as Tony Blair is doing, is INSANE and Anti-Christ." http://christianpost.com/Intl/Overseas/2007/10/evangelicals-have-nothing-to-fear-from-islam-says-european-leader-20/index.html (accessed April 14, 2009).

[98] Volf, 118.

Living Our Lives in the Light of the Cross

If Christians would live a more authentic, biblical life in a pluralistic society where Islam is growing, Muslims could be drawn to the truth of the Gospel as lived out by their Christian friend. Pawson ends the epilogue of his book *The Challenge of Islam to Christians* with a quote from Nietzsche, who said: "I want to be saved if Christians looked more saved" and writes: "Muslims must not be allowed to make the same observation if we are to earn the right to share our faith with them."[99]

Sharing the Gospel in the Way of the Cross

The attitude of Christian witness among Muslims needs to reflect the truth of the Gospel.[100] A great stumbling block for Muslims is the cross, because it models the vulnerability of God. In the words of Nickel, "it is crucial that Christians model and interpret the cross."[101]

Willing to Bear the Scandal of the Cross

It has been pointed out earlier in this dissertation that the divine self-giving love manifested on the cross lies at the heart of the Christian faith and should guide one's thinking and behavior towards Muslims. Instead of excluding them from one's societies, communities, and hearts, the heavenly Father has given Christians the example of embracing those that are unlovable, wrongdoers, or even enemies.

But does this work in a world of self-centered human beings, where violence reigns, where sin abounds. Is it not naïve to give

[99] Pawson, 91.

[100] Nickel, 17. Nickel writes that "the Muslim setting repeatedly raises the question of whether the manner of Christian witness matches the content of the gospel message."

[101] Nickel, 11. Nickel believes that "the genius of the early church was the ability to hold together open proclamation of the good news with a peaceable manner of living and speaking and suggests we follow in their footsteps in our encounter with Muslims."

oneself to Muslims, to welcome them, to readjust one's identity in order to make space for them? Will it not be abused; will one not loose oneself in the process?[102] Volf states that this is indeed a strong possibility, but also that there is no other way: "there is no genuinely Christian way around the scandal. In the final analysis, the only available options are either to reject the cross and with it the core of the Christian faith or to take up one's cross, follow the Crucified—and be scandalized ever anew by the challenge."[103]

When the Church in Europe follows the Crucified in serving him among Muslims, Christians need to live their lives in the light of the cross, share the Gospel in the way of the cross, and be willing to live the scandal of the cross and to encourage others to do the same. This could result in Muslims coming to worship the Crucified as the Lord and Savior. One needs the renewing work of the Holy Spirit in one's hearts, because only the Holy Spirit e can replace a spirit of fear with that of grace and love in the midst of hostility.[104]

In the next chapter I will present some instruments the Spirit might be using to replace an attitude of fear with one of grace.

[102] Volf calls this the scandal of the cross. "The ultimate scandal of the cross is the all too frequent failure of self-donation to bear positive fruit: you give yourself to the other—and violence does not stop but destroys you; you sacrifice your life—and stabilize the power of the perpetrator. Though self-donation often issues in the joy of reciprocity, it must reckon with the pain of failure and violence. When violence strikes, the very act of self-donation becomes a cry before the dark face of God. This dark face confronting the act of self-donation is a scandal." Volf, 26.

[103] Volf, 26.

[104] Musk points out that with his help, "Christ's mind can become ours as we get to know the 'Muslim fundamentalist,' our fellow human being. From a secure servanthood might arise creative ways of sharing the heart of the gospel with people for whom that heart is a missing and much-needed centre." Musk, *Holy War*, 18.

Chapter Three
Helping Christians to Overcome their Islamophobia

The way one looks at Islam determines one's willingness or lack of willingness to share one's life with Muslims and also determines one's motive for doing so. I have shown that the main attitude of the average Christian in Europe towards Islam and Muslims is fear, flowing out of the sin of exclusion and resulting in social exclusion. I have also pointed out that instead of fear, a culture of embrace, an attitude of grace, and a behavior modeled on the cross should be the trademark of followers of Jesus Christ in their relationships with Muslims.

This chapter looks at nine books and seven courses that are written and developed to encourage Christians to relate to Muslims in order to find out whether they sufficiently deal with these issues.[1]

Based on the findings in the previous chapter, I suggest that materials that (1) implicitly or explicitly address the attitude of fear; (2) present an open view of Islam as opposed to a closed one (which is one of the characteristics of *Islamophobia*), and (3) encourage Christians to enter into dialogue with Muslims would be the most helpful to encourage Christians to share their lives with Muslims. In order to find out whether the researched materials meet these criteria, I looked at them through three grids, namely:

[1] These books and courses are by no means the only materials written with this purpose in mind, but they are a good representation of what is available at the moment, coming from different perspectives on Islam, different countries and denominational backgrounds. Not all courses and books that are discussed here are written specifically with the European context in mind. Nevertheless, even those materials that are written for other contexts are used quite extensively by churches, schools and Christians throughout Europe which merits their inclusion in this analysis. More background details of the materials are found in Appendix 2.

(1) whether the material presents an open or closed view of Islam; (2) whether the material encourages the reader/student to enter into dialogue with Muslims as part of his or her being a witness of Jesus Christ or whether it focuses on an apologetic approach; or (3) whether the material not only gives information about Islam but also addresses the Christian's attitude towards Muslims.

An Open or Closed View of Islam

Introduction

I have stated in the previous chapter that a closed view of Islam is one of the characteristics of *Islamophobia.* I have also listed some characteristics of such a closed view of Islam. The Runnymede Trust gives the following characteristics of an open view of Islam:

1) Islam is seen as diverse and progressive, with internal differences, debates and development,
2) Islam is seen as interdependent with other faiths and cultures—(a) having certain shared values and aims (b) affected by them, or (c) enriching them,
3) Islam is seen as distinctively different, but not deficient, and as equally worthy of respect,
4) Islam is seen as an actual or potential partner in joint cooperative enterprises and in the solution of shared problems,
5) Islam is seen as a genuine religious faith, practiced sincerely by its adherents,
6) Criticisms of 'the West' and other cultures are considered and debated,
7) Debates and disagreements with Islam do not diminish efforts to combat discrimination and exclusion,
8) Critical views of Islam are themselves subjected to critique, lest they be inaccurate and unfair[2]

[2] The Runnymede Trust, *Islamophobia: A Challenge for Us All*, 5.

Fear and prejudice are often based on stereotypes, which come out of a closed view of Islam. A closed view considers Islam a monolithic bloc, and fundamentalist Muslims are made representative of the whole of Islam. An open view of Islam would emphasize the social, linguistic, national, and ethnic differences among Muslims. Material that favors an open view of Islam emphasizes the idea of relating to Muslims as people and individuals, as communities, and how Islam is practiced in daily life, rather than simply learning about ideal Islam. An open view would encourage serious and sympathetic study of Islam and emphasize understanding Islam at its best. An open view stimulates Christians to read what Muslims write about their own faith. Material with an open view of Islam encourages Christians to enter into the world of Islam with sympathy or empathy and to get inside the mind and heart of Islam and get the feel of it in order to be at home within it.

Following is a brief analysis of the materials. The materials have been divided into four categories: (1) those with a predominantly closed view of Islam; (2) those with a somewhat closed view on Islam; (3) those with a mostly open view of Islam, but with pockets of a closed view; (4) materials with an open view of Islam. The materials with an open view of Islam have been subdivided into three categories: (a) those that are critical but respectful; (b) those that look for the person behind the Muslim; (c) those that are willing to listen to Muslims and to look for positive aspects of Islam. For clarity's sake, the evidence and examples of the conclusions are found in the footnotes.

Materials with a Predominantly Closed View of Islam

The course *Engaging with Islam*[3] strengthens the stereotype that Islam is an aggressive religion that attacks Christianity and seeks world domination. Constantly the course gives the students

[3] Samuel Green, *Engaging With Islam: A Training Course for Christians* (Kingsford, Australia: Australian Fellowship of Evangelical Students, 2006).

the impression that Islam enters Western countries, promotes the good of Islam, attacks Christian doctrine, and seeks to Islamizing Western societies. The course encourages Christians to defend themselves against such Islamization. The material paints a one-sided picture of Islam with the emphasis on an ideal Islam, and hardly anything is said about individual Muslims.[4]

The *Training Materials of Life Challenge Africa*[5] depicts primarily the view of original Islam as seen from its sources. Nowhere in the material is Islam given a personal face. The emphasis is clearly on Islam as a religion.[6] The material (1) compares the worst in Islam with the best of Christianity;[7] (2) paints a predominantly negative picture of Islam;[8] and (3) fails to differentiate differences among Muslims and makes general statements.[9]

[4] Although in session 3, Green mentions that Islam has many faces and therefore we have to be careful to say "Muslims believe this," in the remainder of the session and the course he looks at how Mohammed practiced Islam and how the books (Qur'an, Hadith) define Islam.

[5] Gerard Nehls and Walter Eric, *Reach Out and Trainers's Textbook* (Nairobi, Kenya: Life Challenge Africa, 2006).

[6] The inside cover of TT 1, indicates that this course teaches Islam a) as it sees itself; b) as others see it; c) as it is. This last remark suggests that there is something as an objective view on Islam and that one finds it in this material.

[7] One of the stated objectives of the course is that Christians can "honestly and graciously answer the Muslims' often offensive attacks on our Lord Jesus Christ, the Bible and the Church." (Introduction of Reach Out) This presumes that Christians are gracious and Muslims are offensive, without considering the possibility that it can also be the other way round.

[8] Islam is presented as a powerful intruder (Reach Out, 1), attempting to make Africa the first Islamic continent (Reach Out, 12), unashamed in its use of force (TT2, 103,104), militant (TT3,43). The Sword of Muhammad and the Qur'an are presented as "the most fatal enemies of civilization, liberty and truth which the world has yet known" (TT3, 96).

[9] The material writes that "Muslims" totally refuse to recognize the need to subject the Qur'an and the Hadith to scholarly scrutiny and evaluation (TT1, 54); are very vocal to make known their demands regarding Muslims living in non-Muslim countries, but not prepared to grant similar rights to Christians living in an Islamic context (TT3,42); have a way of jumping from subject to subject, when they feel they cannot deal with a topic, and rather defend themselves by attacking the Bible.(TT3,68);have no deep spirituality in their lives (TT3, appendix, 128); are slaves of a system, that indoctrinated them (TT2, 103,104, TT3, 21, TT3, 33)

The book *Islam: The Challenge to the Church* focuses on standard Islam[10] and throughout the book the author makes stereotypical statements.[11] The author regularly compares the beautiful ideas of Christianity with the practices of Islam.[12]

Materials with a Somewhat Closed View on Islam

The book *Muslims and Christians at the Table*[13] regularly makes stereotypical and generalized statements and fails to point out the variety of opinions among Muslims in the United States.[14] Sometimes the book compares the realities of Islam with the ideals of Christianity.[15] Occasionally the authors make unfounded value

[10] Patrick Sookhdeo, *Islam: the Challenge to the Church* (Wiltshire, UK: Isaac Publishing, 2006). Although he acknowledges that there is a wide diversity of opinion within Islam, and numerous divisions, sects and movements, the author's rationale for focusing on standard Islam is stated in his preface "Despite this there is a core orthodoxy which is fairly easy to identify and it is this 'standard' Islam which will be our main focus", 6.

[11] One reads that a typical Muslim believes that "their faith must impact the society in which they live and must contribute to the Islamic character of that society" (10). It is pointed out that "a relatively few liberal Muslims adapt their faith to integrate modern society" (10). One reads that a Muslim man may have up to four wives, but it is not pointed out that in several Muslim countries polygamy is forbidden by law, and most Muslims in the West are not able or willing to have four wives. One reads that "protective deceit and dissimulation are an intrinsic part of Islam," with the result that "what is said in English to Christians one day might be totally contradicted the next day by the same leaders" (33).

[12] He writes that "contrary to Christianity, it is shame rather than guilt which is the guiding principle in Islam" (30). This insertion is not true. Others (e. g. Roland Muller) have pointed out that guilt, as much as shame and power are all found in the Bible as consequences of sin, which are addressed in the Gospel.

[13] Bruce McDowell and Anees Zaka, *Muslims and Christians at the Table* (New Jersey: P & R Publishing Company, 1999).

[14] They write that "the Muslim community has five primary goals in the United States" (23), that "Muslims are seeking to become politically involved in America, ultimately to Islamize the country" (24) and that "the fifth and final step for Muslims in America is to develop *da'wah*" (25). Also they make sweeping statements such as "war and the use of force were incorporated as a doctrine of faith" (39) and Islam "developed into a means for military conquests" (41).

[15] The question is asked: "How could you present a Christian view of marriage to your Muslim friend that would be more attractive than Muhammad's model? (48)". In chapter 8, the biblical ideal of the Kingdom of God as expressed by Jesus is compared

judgments, without giving Muslims an opportunity to present their case.[16]

Materials with a Mostly Open View of Islam, But with Pockets of a Closed View

Developing a Heart for Muslims[17] is mostly value-free and generally reflects a fair attitude towards Islam. Unfortunately, there are pockets of clearly negative, stereotypical language in this course.[18] When dealing with Israel and the situation in the Middle East, the material loses its neutrality and clearly takes a pro-Israel and anti-Arab stand.[19]

with a vision statement about the growth of Islam in present-day America (145), instead of with how Christians implement the vision of the Kingdom in today's America.

[16] "Although the Qur'an asserts otherwise, it is a very difficult book for contemporary readers to understand." (72) Sometimes the way information is given is biased and one-sided, for instance: "The rise of Islamic fundamentalism has generated a renewed interest in women wearing a head covering" (51), ignoring the fact that immorality in Western societies is also a reason for this. After explaining that Muslims do not eat pork and pork products, we read that "however, some Muslims raise pigs to sell to non-Muslims" (51), which could easily be understood as considering Muslims insincere.

[17] Cartor Dos, ed., *Developing a Heart for Muslims: an introduction to Islam* (Atlanta: C. A. M. E. L, 2007).

[18] On their website (http://www.anintroductiontoislam.com/Seminars.htm) one reads that the central theme of the material is *"Dealing With the New Goliath: ISLAM."* One learns that the Muslims in the US are controlled by one of the most radical Islamic groups around, that has the same goal as in Europe, namely to subjugate, Arabize and Islamize a nation. In the material one reads that "tens of millions of Muslims have moved to Europe, so much so that many Muslims call it Eurostan" (89, 90). The last article of the last session, entitled *Islam in the light of Scripture*, is full of negative, stereotypical language. It speaks of "the oppressive belief of Islam" and mentions that "mosques are going up virtually daily in the Western world." Islam is called "an unforgiving and uncompromising system, even though it may outwardly appear to be quite accommodating. Islam's intolerance of other religions demonstrates itself in a disturbingly violent manner." The article refers to Muslim leaders killing people who convert to Christ, and considers Islam "still as uncompromising and fearful as it has ever been." On the DVD that comes with the course, one finds a video clip of terroristic activities with the background sound of repeatedly calling Allahu Akbar. Another video clip shows a stoning ceremony in Iran.

[19] To explain the negative attitude of Muslims towards the state Israel the material points to Muhammad's negative attitude towards the Jews. "Mohammad's attitudes to-

Materials with an Open View of Islam

Materials that are Critical but Respectful

The book *Grace for Muslims*[20] wants to help readers develop a more nuanced understanding of Islam. Although the author writes very positively about Islam and Muslims, he does not deny the dark side of Islam.[21] When talking and writing about Islam, the author seeks to do so in accordance with the words of John Chrysostom: "People who love interpret the facts about the one they love much more accurately than those who do not love. Because our eyes have seen badly we have only noticed the darker aspects."[22] The author finds echoes of grace in the Qur'an.[23] When addressing the core issues where Islam disagrees with Christianity, the author believes it is helpful to ask what Muhammad's original intention was and how it was intended to guide the Muslim.[24]

The information given about *Islam in Carey Course in Christian-Muslim Relations*[25] is neutral and value-free. The material

wards the Jews as expressed in the Qur'an have not helped in the matter. One could interpret the Qur'an as anti-Jewish" (93). This might be true, but the reality is that not every Muslim interprets the Qur'an in this way.

20 Steve Bell, *Grace for Muslims? The journey from fear to faith* (Milton Keynes: Authentic Media, 2006).

21 The author expresses his anger with Muslims who are engaged in politicized Islam and differentiates them from the ordinary Muslims. He mentions that there are over 100 violent *jihadic* passages in the Qur'an and 109 passages urging war in the name of Islam. (44), but points out that "Christians need to recognize that... there are violent passages in the Old Testament which also need careful explanation" (e. g. Gen. 34, Josh. 7; 8:1–39; Judges 20; 1 Sam. 15: 1–5) (45).

22 Ibid.15.

23 The place of Abraham in Islam; and the similarity between the Islamic understanding of God and the more austere passages in the Old Testament. The author believes that almost all Islamic tenets of faith and practice are biblical themes. (62–68)

24 Ibid., 80.

25 Dr. Elsie Maxwell, ed., *Carey Course in Christian-Muslim Relations* (London: London Bible College, 2001). For example when addressing Islam in Britain, the material makes the student aware of the missionary activities of some Muslims, but presents it in a balanced, non-hysterical way and compares these activities with those of Christians. In study topic 14, one of the activities given is: "How are Muslims using their jobs to serve

regularly refers to Islamic sources and encourages Christians to look at matters from the perspectives of their Muslim friends and put themselves in their shoes.[26] When writing about Islamic practices and convictions, the material uses words like *many* Muslims, *some* Muslims, *most* Muslims, a *few* Muslims etc., leaving room for variations.

Materials that Look for the Person Behind the Muslim

The book *Ask your Muslim Friend*[27] makes a distinction between Islam as a religion and Muslims as people. Although the book gives basic information about ideal Islam, the author emphasizes the fact that one needs to view Muslims as individuals and Christians are encouraged to differentiate between facts and wishful thinking of Muslims.[28] The author points out that one should

the cause of Islam in your area? Do you know any Christians who are doing the same to teach Muslims for Christ?" (II, 84) The study topic on Muhammad gives a lot of information about his life and background and the student is encouraged to reflect on this in the light of Scripture, but the material itself does not draw a conclusion it only says: "There are questions which can be raised about the lifestyle of Muhammad and about his claims to prophethood." (I, 11) When talking about the Qur'an, the material points to contradictions in the Qur'an but doesn't draw explicit conclusions from it, but merely states: "Again one might ask why are there these contradictions in a book which make claims to be of superior linguistic style and beauty, coming directly from God?" (I, 23).

[26] Ibid., II, 92. It also states that to understand Islam from a Muslim's point of view "you should read books which Muslims write for other Muslims" (II, 94) and the student is given some examples of some of these books and then the material concludes with "a study of easily obtainable books like these, will be a start to understanding the present goals and teachings of Islam. Muslim neighbors will have been influenced by such ideas" (II, 94).

[27] Andreas Maurer, *Ask your Muslim Friend* (Edleen, South Africa: AcadSA Publishing, 2008).

[28] In his basic rules for witnessing to Muslims he encourages to view Muslims as normal human being and as individuals, differing from each other. He points out that we should avoid viewing them in a stereotypical way, because each Muslim follows his own form of folk-Islam which he practices differently to others (133,134). He describes the various groups and movements within Islam and states that "each individual Muslim lives out the kind of faith he is born into and which he adapts during his life, mixing it with local customs and culture" (85).

not assume that one knows what Muslims believe and therefore we should ask questions.

The author of the book *The Crescent through the eyes of the Cross*[29] encourages his readers to try to stand in the shoes of Muslims and see things from their perspective.[30]

The book *Distinctly Welcoming*[31] points out that as one encounters people of other faiths, one should look at the human behind the religion.[32] The author encourages the readers to learn more and find out more about the faiths of other people through asking, visiting, enquiry and listening.[33]

The author of the book *The Call of the Minaret* wants to discover the meaning of Islam for Muslims. He considers a Muslim not as a subject having captivating thoughts and feelings, as part of a picture created for a tourist, but as "a man in earnest; a voice with an imperative... and the more fully we do him justice, the more inevitably we involved him, and so ourselves, in the significance of Christ."[34]

[29] Nabeel T. Jabbour, *The Crescent Through the Eyes of the Cross* (Colorado Springs, USA: NavPress, 2008).

[30] He writes: "I wish you could meet all my Muslim friends. In this book, I will attempt to convey to you how they feel and what they think. Since it is impossible for you to meet all of them, I have invented Ahmad... he is not one person but a composite of many Muslims I know. But he is very real, and the things he has to say will help us understand how Muslims feel about us."(27)

[31] Richard Sudworth, *Distinctly Welcoming* (NSW, Australia: Scripture Union Australia, 2007).

[32] The author points out that it is vital that one sees beyond the label "Hindu," to see a mother, called Sarita, that one discovers the hardworking student Mohan in the Sikh, or the devoted husband Ajahn in the Buddhist. "Ultimately let us aim to find the friend in the person of another faith, as did Jesus, our pattern, model and source." (152)

[33] He writes that when researching another faith, one needs to be open to the beliefs of others, and seek authoritative sources from that other faith "The best research is a combination of study, reading, internet browsing and personal asking, visiting, enquiry and listening; because textbooks will only help us part of the way." (87)

[34] Kenneth Gragg, *The Call of the Minaret* (Oxford: Oxford University Press, 1956), 174, 184.

Materials that are Willing to Listen to Muslims and to Look for Positive Aspects of Islam

The material of *Friendship First: the manual* points out that "Christ, in his dealings with ordinary people around him, tended to free them from the 'ideal' religion of the professionals." The students are asked to reflect on his/her positive and negative stereotypes of Islam. After pointing out that "a Muslim is not a Muslim is not a Muslim," it lists various differences among Muslims. The information about Islam is stated as neutrally and as positively as possible.[35]

The course *Encountering the World of Islam* states that "Christians should listen to Muslims, because Muslims explain their views better than we ever could." The material includes articles written by Muslims. When discussing the person of Muhammad the material recognizes his strengths and judges him by the light of the time in which he lived, rather than by our present-day standards. The student is asked to reflect on what benefits Islam brought into the cultures and civilizations and what makes Islam attractive.[36]

The author of the book *Faith to Faith* seeks to be sensitive towards Islam and uses Muslim sources to make his point. He avoids making hasty judgments about Muhammad and judging the religious lives of individual Muslims. The book breathes an atmosphere of respect into Islam and Muslims and readers are encour-

[35] Steve Bell, *Friendship First: the Manual* (Market Rasen, UK: Friendship First Publications, 2003), 8, 15, 16, 18, 19. The student is encouraged to find things that are good and just in Islam (20). On page 26–28 the material lists several appealing aspects of Islam.

[36] Keith E. Swartley, ed., *Encountering the World of Islam* (Colorado Springs: Authentic Publishing, 2008). See page xxvii. In lesson 4, one is encouraged "to listen to our Muslim friend's opinion, and respond to his or her needs, while not giving in to responding or thinking in terms of stereotypes." (118) The course includes an article by the Royal Embassy of Saudi Arabia in the US on *Islam and the Development of Knowledge*, and a Muslim author writes about the *Fundamental Articles of Faith in Islam*.

aged to be careful not to dismiss any truth in Islam or any evidence of God's grace at work in the life of Muslims.[37]

The book *Cross and Crescent* seeks to understand Islam from the inside and points out that Christians have no right to say what is real or true Islam.[38]

Dialogue or Apologetic Approach to Muslims

Introduction

I have argued in the previous chapter that dialogue is the key to overcoming *Islamophobia*, because it helps to know the other better and to see as the other sees. Dialogue involves meeting with Muslims. Fear and prejudice towards Islam and Muslims are often strongest in those who hardly have personal contact with Muslims. Therefore, materials that help Christians deal with their *Islamophobia* should encourage them to meet Muslims face to face and help them to relax and feel at ease in the company of Muslims. Materials of this kind should not only deal with an apologetic approach and teach Christians how to answer Muslim objections as to how to defend the Christian faith and how to persuade Muslims

[37] Chawkat Moucary, *Faith to Faith: Christianity and Islam in Dialogue* (Nottingham: Intervarsity Press UK, 2001). He writes: "In order to minimize the risks of an unfair comparison between Christianity and Islam I have deliberately based my study of these religions on their respective Scriptures... I have tried to present the Qur'anic message as it is understood by Muslims themselves, more specifically Sunni Muslims" (17). He states his rationale for avoiding hasty judgments as follows: "Not recognizing Islam as a God-given religion does not imply a value judgment on a Muslim's religious life. God loves and cares for all he has made; he is at work in the lives of all his human creatures regardless of their religious background. Many Christians do not live up to the teaching of the Gospel any better than Muslims follow the teaching of the Qur'an" (269). The author believes that Christians must be prepared to learn from Muslims and if, need be, to have their views about them challenged. They should listen carefully to Qur'anic criticisms, which in some cases may be justified. (271, 272)

[38] Colin Chapman, *Cross & Crescent: responding to the Challenge of Islam* (Downers Grove, IL., USA: IVP Books, 2007). The author writes that "one way of learning to appreciate Muslim culture is to allow Muslims to explain their culture in their own words" (32).Also he points out that "Islam is what Muslims say it is."(59)

to read the Bible, but go beyond the arguments and counter-arguments and have eye and ear for the human behind the Muslim. In this light one would also expect such materials to address issues that are broader than just issues related to the spiritual side, such as racism, minority rights, discussion on matters regarding integrating Muslims in Western societies, etc.

Following is a brief analysis of the materials. The materials have been divided into eight categories: (1) materials that are silent about meeting with Muslims and predominantly negative about dialogue; (2) materials that are ambivalent about meeting with Muslims and somewhat polemical; (3) predominantly apologetic material; (4) materials that are positive about dialogue, but do not explicitly encourage meeting with Muslims; (5) materials that favor dialogue and encourage Christians to meet with Muslims; (6) materials that encourage Christians to meet with Muslims and that are positive about an apologetic approach, although also open to dialogue; (7) materials that encourage meeting with Muslims and that favor dialogue about apologetic; (8) materials that seek to balance witness with dialogue. For clarity's sake, the evidence and examples of the conclusions are found in the footnotes.

Materials that are Silent about Meeting Muslims and Negative about Dialogue

The course *Developing a Heart for Muslims* does not encourage students to meet with Muslims. It does not deal with methods or evangelism and it hardly provides Christians with tools on how to share the Gospel with Muslims. Neither apologetics nor dialogue is given much thought. When the course speaks about dialogue, it is in a very negative way.[39]

[39] E. g. in session six one reads that "God's people must be aware of the fact that many so-called Christians are willing to compromise the Truth of God's Word in the attempt to 'build bridges' with various religions... Rather than witnessing to these lost souls, ecumenical leaders are encouraging Christians to search for common ground with Muslims. Instead of exposing the errors of Islam, Christians are told to search for the

Materials that are Ambivalent about Meeting Muslims and Somewhat Polemical

The book *Islam: The Challenge to the Church* is ambivalent about meeting with Muslims. After twenty pages of warnings and critical discussion of eight ways in which Christians interact with Muslims, the author writes that "none of the above cautions about Christian-Muslim relations should prevent Christians from seeking to make friends with Muslims . . ."[40]

The book discusses several issues related to Islam (and especially its presence in the West) such as legislation, education, role of women, media, and politics in a polemical way.[41] The book argues against Christian-Muslim cooperation on none- religious projects, relief, development, and aid.[42] The author is very critical of dialogue and of those that look for commonalities between Islam and Christianity.[43]

truth in Islam. While 'Christians' are patting themselves on the back for their 'open mindedness,' Muslims are spreading their false religious propaganda under the cover of 'dialogue.' "

40 Sookhdeo, 90. This is a bit odd, because he cautions against building friendships, listing the several blocks and complications that come our ways when trying to do so, such as the theology of Islam prohibiting Muslims of having Christian friends, the Muslim *fatiha* prayer including God's anger against Christians; Muslims speaking of those outside Islam as *kafir*; Muslims being generous givers in gifts and hospitality, but reluctant receivers (71–74).

41 He states that Muslims "are quick to seize upon any available legislation to try to attack any perceived slighting of Islam." (Sookhdeo, 56). Also that Muslims "are making use of Western education systems to present a favorable image of Islam to the West."(Sookhdeo, 57)

42 See pages 83–88. The author states that "Christians should first gain a realistic knowledge of the nature of Islam, its agenda and how Muslims view their relationship with Christians" (Sookhdeo, 84).

43 He believes this approach does not suit Islam. "Focusing on aspects of religious phenomena in Islam which are apparently held in common with Christianity does not lead to a correct understanding of Islam" (6). On pages 80–83 he points out to the risks involved and states that most Christians involved in dialogue have no intention of persuading the Muslims with whom they are speaking to become Christians. He suggests that the small number of Christians who use dialogue as a starting point for evangelism, should describe these as discussion meetings.

Predominantly Apologetic Material

The course *Engaging with Islam* is apologetic in nature from beginning to end, and sometimes very polemic.[44] The emphasis is on theological issues. Only at the end of the course, students are encouraged to speak with Muslims.[45]

The *Training Material of Life Challenge Africa* does not explicitly encourage the students to meet with Muslim friends, neighbors or contacts.[46] The emphasis is on informing Christians about Islam and comparing Islamic and Christian doctrines and helping Christians share their faith with Muslims. Other matters that concern Muslims as human beings are not addressed. A lot of emphasis is put on apologetics and it is pointed out that there is no way to bypass apologetics when sharing the Gospel meaningfully with Muslims.[47] The material speaks against replacing debates with dialogue

[44] At the end of session 3, Green says: "In the end we have something better to offer than what Islam brings. All the Islamic doctrines ultimately fail, because they don't have the doctrine of the Gospel. Our task as Christians is to understand Islamic doctrine, so we can stand our ground and then to move forward and to present the Gospel to the Muslims." In the fourth session he discusses reasons Muslims give of Mohammed being a prophet and finds these faulty. He concludes that Mohammed is not a true prophet. In session five, he lists arguments Muslims use to promote Islam and finds them wrong.

[45] After finishing the course, under the heading *What to do next,* people are encouraged to talk to Muslims with the admonition "Don't be afraid. Trust God and talk to them as you would anyone else. Most Muslims are quite reasonable and keen to discuss things." (59). In the last session the student is encouraged to get to know the person (i. e. Muslim) he is talking to and to take an interest in them, but throughout the course one constantly hears and reads of "them", "they," "Islam," "Muslims" in a general, abstract, non-personal sense.

[46] Of the sixty one questions for further study and reflection in Reach Out, only one question encourages the student to meet with a Muslim, namely "Find out what fears influence the life of your Muslim friend. How could they overcome these fears in their life." The rest of the questions are mostly to reproduce the content of the course.

[47] Teacher's Training Manual 2 mostly deals with an apologetics. One learns that sharing the Gospel with Muslims also means defending, because "most Muslims will immediately challenge our beliefs." (Nehls, TT2, 1). In Reach Out (Nehls, 71, 72), Christians are encouraged to learn to argue with Muslims about spiritual matters. Although the material endorses such an approach, it is against having an argument that is conducting verbal fist-fights with Muslims about God or the Bible.

and mutual tolerance and an approach that considers what unites Christians and Muslims instead of emphasizing the differences.[48] It disapproves of life-style evangelism and a demonstration approach, which is considered a silent, timid witness.[49] The course links dialogue with liberal Christianity and believes it could become counterproductive to effective evangelistic witness.[50] The material seeks to encourage Christians to overcome their fear of Muslims by providing them with rational and factual arguments.[51]

Materials that are Positive about Dialogue, but Do Not Explicitly Encourage the Student to Meet with Muslims

The bulk of the book *Faith to Faith* deals with theological and doctrinal differences between Muslims and Christians. In addition the book addresses two other issues that impact Christian-Muslim

[48] "For a Christian to shrink back from explaining what he believes and why he believes, will be interpreted as weakness, uncertainty or ignorance by the Muslim enquirer." (Nehls, TT2, 101, 102)

[49] Against Christians who believe that the use of apologetics, reasoning, proclaiming or explaining spiritual content leads to controversial debates or polemics and who opt for a demonstration approach, the material states that this is not perceived by Muslims "as a display of humility, but rather weakness." The course states that to avoid the use of apologetics altogether in favor of displaying a Christian lifestyle in humility and love to attract Muslims to Christ is "simply based on the false assumption that Muslims think like Christians. Christian life-style without a clearly defined presentation of the Savior Jesus Christ is no witness at all." (Nehls, TT3, 57)

[50] The reason given for this is that" when dialogue is translated into an exchange of thoughts and religious experiences, or "ecumenical" prayers jointly performed by leading representatives of various religions, the signal given is that of acceptance of the divine origin of these." The conclusion is that "we cannot avoid presenting the Christian message over against Islam. That means that we have to expose the origin, roots and deficiencies of Islam at some time or other. When and how this must be done is a sensitive matter, but to avoid it will mean that a Muslim will never be convinced in his heart and that he must turn away from Islam to become part of Christ." (Nehls, TT3, 58)

[51] In the context of discussing polemics between Muslims and Christians, the student is encouraged not to fear "for when rational and factual argument is truly on our side, we need not fear—not for ourselves and much less for God!" (Nehls, TT3, 36)

relations (the Arab-Israeli conflict and the situation faced by immigrants in Europe).[52]

The author's approach to Islam can best be termed apologetic in dialogue or missionary dialogue. He does not want his debate with Muslims to turn into a polemic, "in which one side tries to ridicule, attack and even defeat the other," nor does he want a Christian-Muslim dialogue to be "an attempt to exchange information without any effort to argue for a position." He believes that "while conversion is neither the immediate nor the only aim of dialogue, it must, nevertheless, be accepted as a possible outcome." The author believes that although tolerance is a prerequisite in Christian-Muslim relationships, tolerance should not deny or minimize the theological differences between Christianity and Islam.[53] The author prefers dialogue[54] above a confrontational debate.[55]

The book *The Call of the Minaret* points out that Christian concerns must go beyond the effort of understanding represented by

[52] The author points out that in response to the presence of Muslim immigrants in their countries, some Christians have been tempted to support discriminatory policies. He finds this unacceptable. "Christians should not tolerate any form of racism. Religious racism can be worse than ordinary racism because it dishonors God and is more difficult to eliminate" (Moucary, 283). He believes that Christians should be "among the first to oppose any policy that sets out to discriminate unfairly" (Moucary, 287).

[53] Ibid.,19. Moucary writes: "Christians and Muslims will be genuinely tolerant only when they have accepted the idea that debate, or dialogue, may lead to conversions either to Christianity or to Islam. True tolerance is to accept the other, not by ignoring the distance between us, but by measuring that distance accurately and by recognizing that whoever wants to cross over has the right and freedom to do so" (20).

[54] He points out that dialogue requires our commitment to both truth and love. "... dialogue between Christians and Muslims is a serious business. Its primary concern is the truth about God, ourselves, our fellow human beings and the world in which we live. Political correctness, ignorance or theological relativism may lead to a superficial agreement between us." (Moucary, 21)

[55] A confrontational debate "may run the risk of causing antagonism, which would hinder the search for truth. Only love, demonstrated through genuinely peaceful relationships, can create the necessary conditions for the truth to emerge and for mutual understanding to develop" (Moucary, 21).

the most careful study of books and documents, because the Christian is the ambassador of a person-to-person relationship.[56]

The whole book breathes the air of dialogue, where listening, understanding, and responding is taking place. In chapter 10, the author writes an apologetic and discusses some topics that he considers to be the main ones for our interpretation to the Muslims.[57]

He also states that the misunderstandings that Muslims have about Jesus and other aspects of the Christian faith will be set right, not by argument, but by a constructive effort to discover and correct the sources from which they come.[58]

By introducing his fictitious Muslim friend, Ahmad, to the reader, the author of *The Crescent through the Eyes of the Cross* gives Islam a human face. Grievances, concerns, and objections are put into the mouths of Muslim friends and become personal. Giving Islam a human face helps the readers to put themselves in the shoes of their Muslim neighbor, to learn how they feel, what they think and to look at the world, the West, and Christianity through their eyes.

The whole book is put in a dialogical style in which the author is in dialogue with his Muslim friend and his relatives. When the

[56] Gragg writes that a Christian "must surpass the limits of merely academic knowledge... As the bearer of 'the Word made flesh', he must strive to enter into the daily existence of the Muslims, as believers, adherents, and men." (189) He points out that "We cannot institutionalize the world into God's Kingdom. Nor can we fulfill our ministry except by an intimate relationship with ordinary people... It is our life-task to make bridges into their minds. This means being near enough to be heard; getting near is a large part of our problem" (Gragg, 274)

[57] Such as Christian Scripture, the Person of Jesus, the Cross, the Christian doctrine of God, the Christian church and society. Gragg, 319.

[58] He writes that "assertiveness such as this is not overcome by its like, but rather by the patiently objective. Here are not simply arguments to be refuted: he is a tragedy to be redeemed. What matters is not that men have thought ill of Christianity but that they have forfeited the Christ" (Gragg, 248).

author discusses subjects that are generally used in apologetics, he does so in a respectful manner.[59]

Materials that Favor Dialogue and Encourage Christians to Meet with Muslims

The gracious attitude of the author of the book *Grace for Muslims?* comes through almost on each page of the book and this attitude helps the reader to see Muslims in a more sympathetic light, which could serve as an encouragement to meet Muslims. The author encourages the reader to make a "conscious effort or a purposeful activity to develop a relationship" with Muslims.[60] He differentiates friendship evangelism from relational witness.[61] The book doesn't really go into apologetic, or dialogue. Indirectly, the author seems to argue against an apologetic approach, when he points out that the issue often is not the content or strength of the argument, but the attitude that lies behind the argument.[62]

[59] When writing about possible grammatical, geographical, and historical mistakes in the Qur'an, he states that Muslims have a great challenge to meet, namely "Whose mistakes are they?... The Qur'an has not yet received the scrutiny that the Bible has gone through by Christian theologians... Will the Qur'an be allowed to go through similar scrutiny? If so, will it pass the test?" (Bell, Grace, 179). The author also writes:"As I listened to my friend Ahmad say, "The Qur'an was not written by men. It was dictated by God through an angel," I thought that there is a time and a place to challenge him. Now is not the right time." (Bell, Grace, 181). He doesn't mention when it is the right time.

[60] Bell, *Grace*, Chapter 7.

[61] In that "relational witness is effective in achieving the intended goal of sharing the good news about Jesus but with the added bonus that it helps us to avoid certain problems" (Bell, Grace, 165). One of these problems is an ethical one. "It is harder to maintain integrity if a friendship is merely the mechanism for evangelism." However, "relational witness enables us to facilitate the faith journey of the other person while avoiding the possibility of becoming a spiritual predator." (Bell, Grace, 165). Later he calls relational witness, a 'spiritual friendship' (Bell, *Grace*, 166). He concludes that relational witness is "a relationship that provides the context for Christian witness rather than merely being a tool to achieve it" (Bell, *Grace*, 168).

[62] Bell, *Grace*, 79. He writes: "I am convinced that the Spirit of God is saying to the whole of his church that it is possible for Christian/Muslim relationships to be marked less by doctrinal bickering and more by the gracious spirit of Jesus" (Bell, *Grace*, 140).

The focus of *Friendship First: the manual* is on Muslim people instead of the religion of Islam. It emphasizes the importance of building friendships with Muslims.[63] It considers the apologetic approach as opposite to a polemic approach.[64] The manual particularly promotes proclamatory dialogue.[65]

Materials that Encourage Christians to Meet with Muslims and are Positive About an Apologetic Approach, Although also Open to Dialogue

Many of the questions at the end of each chapter of the book *Muslims and Christians at the Table* encourage the reader to meet with Muslims[66] and the authors give many guidelines for friendship evangelism. The book mentions in passing that Christians can work together with Muslims to deal with secularism and injus-

[63] The author writes: "The first thing to remember is that until you can use the expression 'friend' of a particular Muslim you are not in the best position to discuss the Good News With them ..." (Bell, *Friendship*, 58). "The biggest step in relating the Good News to a Muslim is when we step away from confrontation and towards genuine friendship ... Through friendship with a Muslim we can steer away from old point-scoring attitudes, on both sides. This is a relational approach whereby a Muslim friend can begin from where he or she is and start to unearth the signposts pointing to Jesus that were there all the time, even within Islam" (Bell, *Friendship*, 13).

[64] An apologetic approach is described as "a commitment to teasing out points, which helps us connect with a Muslim rather than push us further apart", while a polemical approach "tends to emphasize differences and contradictions, which promote arguments" (Bell, *Friendship*, 10).

[65] In Appendix 2 proclamatory dialogue is explained. "This is not a theologically liberal stance, which might tempt us to go in search of points of agreement and compromise at all cost. Like the liberal stance, this form of dialogue does involve listening and genuinely trying to understand and learn. However, it differs in that it also involves having something to say (proclaim) in response to what we hear and learn from our Muslim friend." (Bell, *Friendship*, 74) The material finds in Jesus' discourse with the elders in the temple (Luke 2:45, 46) an example of the principle of proclamatory dialogue (Bell, *Friendship*, 61).

[66] E. g. "What steps do you need to take to relate culturally to Muslims? How may it affect how you relate to your Muslim friend at a meal, in your home, in a mosque, or in a church?" (67). Think of a Muslim friend with whom you have a desire to share the gospel. What have you done to develop your friendship? (McDowell, 216).

tice.[67] The emphasis of the book is very much on motives and methods of Muslim evangelism and does not address issues that Muslims living in the United States have to come to grips with. The book addresses several arguments that Muslims have against the Bible and Christian doctrine and give suggestions how to defend ourselves against these.[68] The authors discuss twenty-four methods for reaching Muslims, including debates and dialogue.[69]

The material of *Carey Course in Christian-Muslim Relations* frequently speaks about "Muslim friends" or "Muslim neighbors" and the students are encouraged to discuss the material that is being taught with their Muslim friends. Several methods of Christian witnessing (proclamation, confrontation, dialogue, debate, traditional evangelism, institutional mode, friendship evangelism, contextualization, storying) are discussed.[70] The "method" of debate is divided into discussion, apologetics and polemics, which are all presented as legitimate methods.[71]

[67] McDowell, 162.

[68] For example that the Bible is corrupted, the Trinity, also the argument that Jesus predicted the coming of Muhammad is addressed and several defects in the argument are listed.

[69] They believe debates must be carried out with much prayer and sensitivity in order not to cause unnecessary offense and conclude that it can work in the right context. But it can also lead to acts of violence. They believe dialogue involves listening to each other with respect and frankly witnessing about our faith. It requires humility, respect, openness to new insights, and trust. They advocate so-called Meetings for Better Understanding, which include an oral presentation by a Muslim and by a Christian on a preselected topic, followed by a period of discussion to learn further, correct each other's misconceptions, and gain a better understanding of each other's faith. They believe that the ministry of Jesus provides a model for such meetings and particularly refer to Lukas 4: 16–19; 5: 17–26; 13:10–13. (McDowell, 182).

[70] Regarding confrontation it states that "it can be an offensive method unless handled with great care by an experienced person" (Maxwell, II, 159), regarding dialogue it states that it needs "to set out clearly what the purpose of the dialogue is" and also that dialogue needs careful planning to be effective (Maxwell, II, 159).

[71] The material provides guidelines for holding discussions with Muslims and in reference to the manner in which such discussions should take place, it encourages listening. Also, the student is encouraged to be "winsome, friendly, polite and courteous, self controlled, actively engaging in a constructive conversation." (Maxwell, II, 61)

The author of *Ask your Muslim friend* believes that the best way to learn about Islam is to ask one's Muslim friends. Throughout the book there are over a hundred questions that one can ask their Muslim friend.[72] It deals briefly with political issues and social issues, like marriage and integration of Muslims in Europe. One section is clearly apologetic, and although the author believes that knowledge of apologetics is highly advantageous, he also emphasizes that it is important to understand the Muslim neighbor, his religion, his reasoning, his hopes, and longings "in order to present the message of the Gospel to him in a way that makes sense."[73] He also writes that Christians need to develop approaches compatible with Christian love which encourage a deeper exchange of views and serious reflection. He identifies three levels of interaction between Muslims and Christians.[74]

Apologetics is described as "to speak in defense of, to justify (explaining why such and such is true) materials and facts, organized to give a systematic argumentative discourse in defense of the divine origin and authority of Christianity." (Maxwell, II, 59). One study topic deals with apologetics. It looks at the main objections to Christianity raised by Muslims and suggests possible responses. Referring to 1 Peter 3:15, it states that "the Christian faith and the scriptures can be explained using rational argumentation. Belief is not expected without interaction of the mind in the process though it includes the action of the heart and the will." (Maxwell, II, 59)

Regarding polemics it writes that some believe "that Christians should not engage in polemics. Others accept polemics for specific situations only, or in the written form, not verbally or publicly," (Maxwell, II, 160).

72 For example: why are you a Muslim? (Maurer, 42), what are the marks of a true Muslim? (Maurer, 86), what is the message of Islam? (Maurer, 93), how did the Qur'an become a written text as it exists today? (Maurer, 102), why does the Qur'an reject the crucifixion in one verse (Sura 4:157), whereas it is a fact of history that it was indeed Jesus who was crucified? (Maurer, 110), what does sin mean to you? (Maurer, 121)

73 Maurer, 128.

74 Namely 1) conversational level, where "Christians talk to Muslims so that both can get to know each other better on social or other issues"; 2) working level, where "Christians and Muslims share responsibility for social and humanitarian projects"; 3) missionary level, where "Christians bear witness to Muslims about Jesus Christ as the truth." (Maurer, 130)

Materials that Encourage Meeting Muslims and Favor Dialogue above Apologetic

In the course *Encountering the World of Islam*, friendship with Muslims is strongly encouraged.[75] The assumption is that demonstrating Jesus Christ's love includes addressing all the needs people have.[76] One of the obstacles mentioned in sharing one's faith with Muslims is that one describes one's position in idealized terms without observing one another following these ideals.[77]

The course promotes relational witnessing and is critical of an apologetic approach that overemphasizes the cognitive and focuses primarily on theological facts and knowledge[78] and believes that "our learning how to relate to Muslims through their familial relationships may prove more significant than simply discussing the content of theological beliefs."[79] It considers a confrontational approach to be not very successful and recommends the dialogical model[80] and being an incarnational witness.[81]

[75] Because "Muslims will recognize the truth in our witness when our communication issues from within deep and lasting friendship relations with them."(Swartley,227) We also read that if we want to demonstrate the saving work and power of Christ in our lives," our friends must see it by observing it in our imperfect daily living. This is how relationships work. Words have little meaning without the valid lives to explain them." (Swartley, 159, 160)

[76] Because: "As Christ has transformed us into new beings, our faith, couples with our empathy for our fellow human beings, compels us to reach out in friendship evangelism, and the good deeds which minister to the whole person and the community, by addressing medical, educational, social, economic, and political needs." (Swartley, xxvi)

[77] It is pointed out that what is needed is "to stop trying to convince the other and to disavow the presumption that our lives demonstrate the perfect version of our religion. After all, the lives of most so-called Muslims and Christians do not match their religions' teaching anyway. After making these attitudinal changes, we could relate as peer counterparts." (Swartley, 79, 80)

[78] Being a relational witness "will be a more tangible, more attractive witness than that provided in a 'drive-by-shooting' of logical truth arguments that do not correspond with what Muslims observe in the 'Christian' world." (Swartley, 271)

[79] Swartley, 158.

[80] But the author states that this approach "must not be confused with the syncretistic, universalistic dialogues sponsored by some ecumenical groups. Missionaries do not

The emphasis of the book and course *Cross and Crescent* is on relating to Muslims and understanding them.[82] The reader is encouraged to visit Muslims in their homes or mosque and spend time with them socially. Such visits should be motivated by loving our neighbor without consideration as to where it will lead to.[83] The material also looks at several issues that are faced by Christians who are living alongside Muslims and are interacting with them in different parts of the world.[84]

The material encourages the students to serve alongside Muslims in the community, and work with them in matters like racism, *Islamophobia*, permission to build mosques etc.[85] The material looks at areas of debate and controversy between Muslims and Christians and gives suggestions as to how to best deal with this controversy.

Although the author prefers an approach of dialogue when relating to Muslims[86] the materials discuss the strengths and weak-

surrender their convictions: they affirm them, using a method that permits concomitant growth in understanding of Muslims" (Swartley, 316).

[81] The reader is encouraged to emulate the example of Jesus (John 1:14; Fil. 2:5–8) and to follow the pattern of the apostle Paul (1 Cor. 9), who "modeled incarnational witness in the community" (Swartley, 289). "For us, presenting an incarnational witness among Muslims could start with appreciating their worldview and culture, and learning their language, but primarily we want them to understand who Christ is." The material points to Samuel Zwemer as an example of someone who "verbally attacked Islam in their careers and later became advocates of incarnational witness as they came to understand and appreciate Muslims as their friends" (Swartley, 312)

[82] Chapman, 17. The author believes that "relating to people is more important than acquiring information or mastering new ideas."

[83] Chapman, 29. Because, "if we want to work out in advance where all our meeting and visiting are going to lead, the chances are that there is still something wrong in our own attitudes. In the teaching of Jesus, the command to love our neighbors is prior to the command to go out and make disciples of all nations. It makes little sense to calculate how we are going to share the gospel with our Muslim neighbors if we have not begun to know them, love them and care for them as our neighbors" (Chapman, 29).

[84] Such as educational needs of Muslims in the UK, wearing the veil in France, introduction of *shari'a* law in Nigeria, the process of Islamization in Malaysia.

[85] Chapman, 53–55.

[86] The material provides a model of genuine meeting and dialogue for the relationship between a Christian and a Muslim based on Luke's description of Jesus in the temple at the age of twelve (Luke 2:45, 46). (Chapman, 24, 25).

nesses of more apologetic approaches. The material briefly deals with the question whether it is ever appropriate for Christians to engage in polemics.[87]

Materials that Seek to Balance Witness with Dialogue

The author of the book *Distinctly Welcoming* points out that we need "to make connections before we can present our challenges."[88] A lot of activities in the book encourage the reader to seek relationships with people of other faiths. The kind of apologetics that the author favors is a Christian life lived out in everyday activities.[89]

The book discusses the importance and manner of dialogue and the author is convinced that "now, more than ever, we need to engage in dialogue with other faiths as a part of our mission of reconciliation and peacemaking."[90] The author has made a diagram

[87] In doing so, the author points out the arguments in favor of and against polemics (Chapman, 365, 366). Although he writes that "many Christians will have reservations about polemics", he leaves it up to the reader to draw his/her own conclusion from the arguments given.

[88] Sudworth, 59. He states that he has written this book as a resource to give shape to productive encounters with people of other faiths because "it is genuine relationships which are currently desperately needed between Christians and those of other faiths. Relationships cannot be programmed and replicated, still less packaged in a paint-by-numbers guide" (23).

[89] He points out that although the theology of the Christian faith is different from the theology of other religions, "the vast majority of the world will only know that it is different when it affects how we behave... What makes us different is not simply what we believe but how our beliefs motivate and affect our behavior. What makes us different is how our faith transforms the way we live. Unless we... learn to demonstrate the dynamic and transforming relationship between our beliefs and our behavior, we are in no better position than any other faiths" (Sudworth, 48). Arguing simply about beliefs rarely convinces people of the validity of them. Seeing them in action makes the difference... Jesus did not argue with the rulers of his time about the validity of the kingdom of God; he went about demonstrating the kingdom of God and explaining how to understand it and live it" (Sudworth, 50).

[90] Sudworth, 101.

in which he clarifies the relationship between witness and dialogue.[91]

Emphasis on Knowledge or Attitude

Introduction

The third grid used in this study to analyze the materials that have been written to encourage Christians to share the Gospel with Muslims, is to determine whether the emphasis is on knowledge or on attitude. Each book and training course that instructs Christians about Islam not only passes on a general knowledge about the religion of Islam, but implicitly or explicitly suggests a certain attitude and a distinctive style of thinking and relating to Islam and Muslims. A particular style of thinking and relating can eliminate, decrease or heighten fear for Islam and Muslims.

In order to be more empathetic to Muslims, Christians need to know something about the life of Mohammad, the Qur'an, the development of Islam, the five pillars, Islamic law, Sufism, Folk Islam, Islam in the modern world etc. It is not necessary to know everything about Islam before one crosses the street to talk to a Muslim. It has been pointed out that fear and prejudices against Islam and Muslims have become deeply ingrained in the mind of Europeans, including European Christians. Material that is written to teach Christians about Islam should bring these prejudices and fears to the surface, and help Christians to deal with it in the light of the Word of God through dependence on the power of the Spirit. Such materials should help Christians at a personal and emotional level, and not just at an intellectual level.

[91] "All of us ought to be holding together something of dialogue and witness as we relate to other faiths. In dialogue there is a tendency to secure relationships, while in witness there is a tendency to secure tradition. The author believes that" an authentic encounter with other faiths holds these two poles together; that a truly biblical mission draws from our distinctive and calls us into relationship with our fellow humanity" (Sudworth, 101).

Underneath an analysis of the materials that have been written to encourage Christians to share the Gospel with Muslims with regard to how the deal with knowledge and attitude. The materials have been divided into five categories: (1) Materials that increase an attitude of fear towards Islam; (2) Materials that provide some biased information on Islam and emphasize information over attitude; (3) Materials that show respect to Islam and Muslims and put more emphasis on information than on attitude; (4) Materials that put more information on attitude than on information; and (5) Materials that predominantly address attitude.

Materials that Increase an Attitude of Fear Towards Islam

The course *Engaging with Islam* does not explicitly deal with the issue of overcoming fear of Islam or prejudices against Muslims. In fact, the tone and content heightens fear and prejudices towards Islam and Muslims. Islam is portrayed as the attacker against which Christians need to defend themselves.[92]

The course considers Islam and Christianity to be in battle and in this context it particularly aims at training Christians in two skills: *to contend*, in defense of the Christian faith and *to confront*, in the attack of Islam. Christianity should confront and challenge Islam.[93] The last session of the course deals briefly with fear and love.[94]

[92] At the beginning of the first session, the students are encouraged to make Islam their business, "because Islam makes it our business, because the Qur'an addresses Christians (Sura 4:47) and asks us to believe; Islam actively seeks to convert Christians to become Muslims; Islam preaches a different gospel and it calls on Christians to reject Jesus as the Son of God; Mohammed gave instructions to his followers how to deal with Christians."

[93] Green says: "Whether we like it or not Christianity must confront Islam." He considers the book of Acts a book of confrontation and concludes that "we must not think that there is anything wrong with confrontation" and that "confrontational evangelism to Islam is necessary."

[94] To the question: Why may it be hard for us to love Muslims? The answer is "We may be afraid of them." The question: Where does our power to love come from? is answered as follows: "The power to love comes from the Gospel. The gospel shows God's love for us." The question: How should Christians deal with fear? is answered with ref-

The kind of information that the book *Islam: the Challenge to the Church* gives and the often polemical tone in which it is presented leads to an increase of fear instead of overcoming it.[95] The desire of the author is to help Christians reach out to Muslims with the Gospel "before it is too late."[96] In the conclusion of the book Sookhdeo writes that "If we do not have the courage to speak the truth in love and witness to our faith we shall be like the Church in the early days of Islam which succumbed and was eradicated."[97] Such language seems to increase an attitude of fear on the part of Christians toward Islam and Muslims.

The emphasis of the *Training materials of Life Challenge Africa* is clearly on knowledge. Although attitude is dealt with, it is in an ambivalent way.[98] Throughout the material the importance of a right attitude is emphasized[99] and some specific attitudes such as

erence to 1 Peter 5:7 and Matthew 10:28 and "when fearful we must pray to God and also remember that God is greater than Islam and is to be feared above Islam."

[95] The author who believes "it is possible for faiths to live together in peace, without one subjugating the rest" (Sookhdeo, 2), nevertheless points out that "sections of the church (e. g. North Africa) have disappeared completely in the face of the challenge of Islam" (2), giving the impression that Islam was the cause for the disappearance of the church.

[96] Sookhdeo, 3.

[97] Sookhdeo, 100.

[98] In the appendix of TT3 (Nehls, 122), the student is given suggestions as how to conduct, prepare and evaluate seminars in churches. A new attitude towards Muslims is given as a possible outcome of the seminars (the content of which is the same as that of this course), but this isn't explicitly dealt with in the material.

[99] In TT 2 (Nehls,100), it is pointed out that our Christian witness could be damaged through poor attitudes. We are particularly warned against the spirit of triumphalism, the inclination to demonize and misrepresent Islam, negative and militant attitudes towards Muslims and the students are encouraged to express the attitudes of fairness, patience and gentleness, avoiding quarrels and disputations, being serious about our faith, and being Biblical in our responses. Also in TT 3 (Nehls,65), right attitude is stressed and it is pointed out that "Muslim evangelism that is induced or nourished by a fear of Islam or by a spirit of triumphalism is bound to produce negative results. Even an in-depth-knowledge of Islamic teaching and practice may be (and too often is!) used in an aggressive and destructive manner. A Christian witness will wholeheartedly seek to understand a Muslim and to share "the truth in love" (Nehls, TT3, 65). In the student handbook Reach Out (Nehls, Reach Out, 36), the student is encouraged to check his or her attitude and particularly warned against being crusaders, to fight, bully, preach at them or bulldoze.

empathy, fearlessness and compassion are advocated.[100] After giving some threatening information about Islam, the student is encouraged to respond in love.[101]

Although positive attitudes towards Islam and Muslims are encouraged and negative attitudes are rejected, the overall impression of the material is that it increases an attitude of fear and animosity, despite the intentions of the authors to do otherwise. One of the key ways this course seeks to encourage Christians to deal with their fear of Muslims is by providing them with rational and factual arguments.[102] Although the material is regularly very negative about Islam and Muslims, the student is encouraged to never use the information in these notes as a weapon against Muslims.[103]

[100] Several of the attitudes promoted are: empathy and sensitivity (Nehls, 63), understanding and trust (Nehls, 63) fearlessness (Nehls, 65), compassion (Nehls, 65), courage, humility, faithfulness (Nehls, 66), ability to formulate and communicate (Nehls, 67).

[101] Although both in the TT's and Reach Out the Islamic ambitions for Africa are discussed and we read that "Islam has vowed to make Africa the first Islamic continent and few would dare to keep their eyes closed to the undeniable advances made by Muslims to accomplish that goal" (Nehls, TT1, 46 and Reach Out 12), we are called not to fight our Muslim fellow citizens! We are told not only to tolerate our enemies, but to love them—even when they do not return our love and refuse to come to the Savior! (Nehls, Reach Out, 13) After discussing the call to jihad and the Christians who are martyred by Muslims, the material continues: "Again we would urge the reader not to blame this on the Muslims he comes in contact with. This report was not compiled to blame any person, but to expose a religious system, which is imperialistic, oppressive and deeply anti-Christian (Nehls, TT3, 97), although the next sentence is: "The present setting of Islam in this world is indeed very threatening."(Nehls, TT3, 97)

[102] In chapter 8 of Reach Out, which deals with witnessing to Muslims, the issue of fear is addressed. We read that fear is based on ignorance. "Everybody is scared of snakes. But if I know *how* they behave and react, and what can be done in case of a snake bite, I lose an irrational fear. Knowledge and experience greatly reduce this fear. The same applies to Muslim evangelism. An ignorant Christian, who does not know Islam or Muslims, and is confronted with typical Islamic anti-Christian propaganda, just cannot deal with this. Ignorance causes fear, and fear suppresses evangelism. (Nehls, Reach Out, 50)

In the context of discussing polemics between Muslims and Christians, the student is encouraged not to fear "for when rational and factual argument is truly on our side, we need not fear—not for ourselves and much less for God!" (Nehls, TT3, 36)

[103] Because these are tools to help one understand what Islam is in its essence. "This tool should help you to gently and kindly demonstrate to a Muslim the difference of a life assured of God's favor through Christ's death over against the uncertainty Islam of-

The course *Developing a heart for Muslims* seeks to provide students with in-depth knowledge of Islam, rather than dealing with attitude-related matters.[104] Nevertheless, throughout the material, comments regarding attitude can be found, particularly with reference to fear, love and understanding.[105]

Materials that Provide Some Biased Information on Islam and Emphasize Information over Attitude

The book *Muslims and Christians at the Table* gives a more prominent role to understanding than to attitude. Understanding Islam is considered basic for reaching Muslims with the Gospel.[106]

fers its followers. (Nehls, Reach Out, 36) The first chapter of Reach Out refers to Islamist terrorism, Muslim suicide bombers, assassination of political opponents, death threats against Christians in the Arab world, perception of Islam being a powerful intruder and responses such as fear, anger, hatred, concern, alarmism and curse. In response to this, we are encouraged "to obey Christ in His desire to save all men" and we are reminded that we "are not give a spirit of timidity (fear) but a spirit of power, of love and of a sound mind." (Nehls, Reach Out, 1)

[104] The reason for this might well be that the producers of the course believe that "an in-depth knowledge of Islam and its beliefs and practices is a prerequisite to knowing and conversing with Muslims. Once you understand that Islam is the problem and Muslims are its victims, you will begin to develop a heart for Muslims—a heart of love and compassion." (information on the website).

[105] On the website promoting the course one reads that "rather than fearing Islam, Christians need to develop a heart of love for the victims of Islam—Muslims." In the workbook, the leader's guide and the website, one finds ten reasons why the people who put the material together love Muslims. "We genuinely love Muslims, their kindness and their food... Without a doubt or hesitation we declare our love for the people of Islam." We also read that the course is aimed at "helping adult believers better understand Islam, proclaim their faith, and love their Muslim neighbors and friends." The introduction of the course book writes that "every Muslim is someone whom God loves. Unfortunately, some Christians make the mistake of not praying for Muslims because of their own prejudices or fears. Let us begin in prayer by asking God to give us a heart filled with love and compassion towards Muslims."

[106] In the introduction of part two, the authors write that "in order to minister effectively to Muslims, it is necessary to understand the history of Muhammad's life and the development of Islam, because they are foundational to Muslims' worldview and our ability to relate the gospel to them. (29). And the introduction to part four reads: "We have presented thus far a framework for understanding Islam. With this background, we can work to reach Muslims with the Gospel" (McDowell, 151).

Throughout the book, reference is made to God's love for Muslims and Muslims are regularly referred to as "friends." Also one learns that one's enemy is Satan, not Muslims.[107] The book only explicitly deals with the attitude of Christians towards Muslims when discussing stereotypes.[108] The authors believe that the right approach to Muslim evangelism is an educational one.[109]

Materials that Show Respect to Islam and Muslims and Put More Emphasis on Information than on Attitude

Although the material of *Carey Course in Christian-Muslim Relations* reflects an attitude of respect and sincerity towards Islam and Muslims, and describes Muslims as friends, the emphasis is more on knowledge than on attitude. It is only towards the end of the course that the material addresses the attitude of the Christian towards Muslims more explicitly. Even then, it directed more toward the activities by way of reflection, than in the teaching part of the material.[110] One thing that stands out in this course is that it emphasizes sound knowledge of Islam.[111]

[107] We should regard them as our friends, neighbors, and fellow human beings made in the image of God. We believe that this is God's perspective."(McDowell, xviii)

[108] Namely chapter 3, pages 61–63. It is pointed out that stereotypes are barriers and hindrances in Muslim evangelism. The reader is encouraged to get beyond stereotypes and deal with reality and truth and at the end of the chapter is asked 'what are some of your assumptions about Muslims." (McDowell, 67). In chapter 9, which deals with the theological basis for Muslim Evangelism, the authors write that being God's voice to Muslims," we must be free of any prejudice or antipathy toward them" (McDowell, 162).

[109] "A teaching ministry is needed for both Christians and Muslims in order to remove the misunderstandings on both sides" (McDowell, 67).

[110] In study topic 18, the student is asked to list what they think Muslims are like and to note what Muslims in general think Christians are like. Then they are asked what areas they need to learn more about in order to better understand their Muslim friends (Maxwell, II, 139). In study topic 19, the student is asked: "what is your attitude towards Islam?" (Maxwell, II, 157). The only explicit teaching on attitude is about the Christian's attitude towards culture. (Maxwell, II, 144,145).

At the end of study topic 18 the material refers to the attitude of the Muslim towards the Christian and we read that "the most effective way to form or change a person's at

In *Faith to Faith*, the author examines the attitude that Christians should adopt when debating with Muslims and encourages the readers to examine their attitudes towards Israel and the Arabs as well. One should renounce ignorance and confrontation and make the effort to listen, to explain and to understand.[112] Christians should have a fair attitude to Islam and Muslims.[113] The author believes that relationships between Christians and Muslims in Europe are often antagonistic because of a tarnished image of Islam.[114] Christians should overcome their prejudices and serve as bridge-builders between European nationals and Muslim immigrants because through their faith "they are in a better position to explain Islam to non-Muslims and to help Muslims relate to European culture."[115]

The material found in the book entitled *Ask your Muslim friend* emphasizes that it is important for committed Christians to be ac-

titude or deep-rooted beliefs is through the personal contact of a friend or member of the family... You, as a Christian witness, must provide that initial care and love" (Maxwell, II, 148).

111 At the beginning of the course, one reads that "it is important to realize that those witnessing to Muslims need a sound knowledge of the Muslim faith, heritage and customs..." (Maxwell, I, 1). This sound knowledge is something that comes through the material time and again and is in agreement with the aims of the material, namely "to give information about Islam which will help Christians address Muslim perspectives, questions and challenges." (Maxwell, I, 1)

112 He believes that the Gospel calls Christians to be witnesses for God to Muslims, which means "renouncing ignorance and confrontation" and "making the effort to listen, to explain and to understand" (Moucary, 290). He also states that if mission is in God's *name*, it must be carried out in God's *way*. "This means dialogue, fairness, respect, and the opportunity to respond freely" (Moucary, 290).

113 He bases this on Jesus' command in Matthew 7:12 "So in everything, do to others what you would have them do to you, for this sums up the Law and the Prophets" In his understanding this means "not comparing the ideals of Christianity with the reality of Islam, radical Muslims with moderate Christians or mainstream Christianity with Islamic sects" (Moucary, 17).

114 "Islamic fundamentalism is mistakenly associated with mainstream Islam. Islamic ideologies in some Muslim countries (e.g. Afghanistan, Iran, Saudi Arabia and Sudan) lead many to believe that Islam is a backward and oppressive religion" (Moucary,288).

115 Ibid.

curately informed about Islam, understanding that popular images are often based on misinformation, kindling fear rather than offering help. The book aims to dispel the Christian's fear, prejudice, and wrong attitudes when meeting Muslims. Two-thirds of the book pertains to providing information about Islam and helping Christians answer Muslim objections. The remainder of the book deals with developing relationships with Muslims, which includes developing a right attitude toward Muslims. The book briefly discusses four attitudes that Christians display in their encounters with Muslims: a) the liberal attitude, that considers Islam as valid a way to God as Christianity; b) the adapting attitude, that tries to contextualize the Gospel as much as possible so as to gain better access to Muslims; c) the militant attitude that sees Muslims as enemies and evangelism not as an option; d) the missionary attitude that has a desire to make Muslims into disciples of Jesus Christ. This fourth attitude is the one the author prefers because with this attitude "Christians meet Muslims in the love of God, and respect their culture, while not compromising the Christian message."[116]

Throughout the book *The Call of the Minaret* the author displays an attitude of respect for Islam and Muslims. Among attitudes that he condemns are arrogance and bitterness. Attitudes that author promotes are reverence, honesty, embrace and the will to understand.[117] The author seeks to provide accurate information, but makes clear that being understood by Muslims means to go beyond the most careful study of books and documents and needs to include entering into the daily existence of the Muslims, as believers, adherents, and men.

The author does not deny that being in Islam is a harsh world, "that disallows the Cross and strips the Christian's Master of His most tremendous meanings," but he believes the harshness has to

[116] Maurer, 130.

[117] Gragg, 179–188.

be transcended by those "for whom every antagonism is an opportunity."[118]

Of the twelve lessons of *Encountering the World of Islam*, there isn't one explicitly on attitude. But the Christian attitude to Muslims is mentioned many times throughout the material.[119] The material is critical of an approach to Muslims that focuses primarily on theological facts and knowledge.[120]

Materials that Put More Emphasis on Attitude than on Information

In the book *The Crescent through the eyes of the Cross*, the attitude of fear of Islam and Muslims is addressed right from the beginning.[121] The emphasis of the book is to show the readers the

[118] "For that, precisely, is the heart of the story itself." (Gragg, 178, 179)

[119] In the introduction, one learns that one of the fundamental assumptions that has lead to the putting together of EWI deals with attitude: "We desire to relate to Muslims as equals. We do not believe in engaging them in argument, for they are not our enemies. We do not fear or blame them, or label them as evil... We want to establish a base of understanding and empathy... Where we must evaluate Islam, we have tried to be careful to use the same criteria of criticism we want applied to ourselves... Please evaluate our fairness toward Muslims as compared to Christ's example of justice." (Swartley, xxv and xxvi)

In the introduction one reads that the knowledge acquired from this course is "not as important as the way it will affect your view of Muslims and future interaction with them." (Swartley, xxxi)

In the article *Ten stumbling blocks to reaching Muslims* (lesson 7) the author writes that "many of our efforts are likely to prevent the western church from reaching Muslims, unless we make some drastic changes in our attitudes and conduct" (Swartley, 236). He particularly refers to one's bias toward Israel, insensitive teaching of end-times prophecy, nationalism, loose morals, disdain for Muslims' culture.

[120] "If we are focusing on knowledge, we will be living from our heads rather than living from our hearts. Our interaction becomes abstract and avoids real relational connection." (Swartley, 270)

[121] The author begins his preface with a reference to a sculpture that has two interrelated scenes back to back, separated by a door. One side was a Native American man in a fierce snowstorm, knocking at the door of a log cabin and pleading for refuge and warmth. On the other side of the door was a warm room with a terrified mother holding a shotgun while the woman's frightened three-year-old daughter clung to her dress. The terrified mother was refusing to open the door. The author compares the fear of this woman with the fear of the unknown that Christians often have regarding Muslims

world through the eyes of Muslims. The readers are encouraged to not only listen with their ears, but particularly with their hearts.[122] The goal of the author is to achieve a change of mind in the readers and help them to see that the way Muslims see Christians is very different from how Christians see themselves. In addition the author is encouraging Christians to see the world through Muslim eyes.[123] He then refers to the transformation that Jonah and Peter had to go through when dealing with people outside their own faith community.[124]

The author encourages the reader to bring every thought about Muslims into captivity to the obedience of Christ (in reference to 2 Corinthians 10:3–6) and gives an illustration of how one can practically develop a new chain of thoughts made up of new links to replace the old chain of thought.[125]

[122] When hearing Ahmad talk about Christians and Christianity, the author writes "I anxiously desired to defend or correct some misconceptions on his part, yet I promised God that I would be willing to listen to him with an open mind. I pleaded to God that somehow Ahmad would see Jesus in my attitude of respect, humility, and willingness to listen and learn" (Jabbour, 33).

[123] "I found out that if I am willing to listen and attempt to understand his perspective, it contributes to strengthening the bridge between us. I believe that the stronger the bridge the heavier the truth it can carry. I do not have to agree with Ahmad on all issues, but I can listen to him because I want to stand in his shoes and see the world through his eyes" (Jabbour, 62, 63).

[124] "Because Muslims need to hear the good news of the gospel, we might see ourselves as superior, since we are the bearers of the message and they are the recipients. We might be so preoccupied with their need that we miss out on what God wants to do in our lives. Like Jonah, we might be blind for our need for transformation." (Jabbour, 97) In reflecting on this chapter, the reader is asked "What kind of transformation do you need in order to have a healthy attitude towards Muslims?" (Jabbour, 97)

In the last paragraph of the book, the author again turns to the book of Jonah and states that "his prayer revealed his rotten attitude and the great need he had to be converted—to repent and to have a heart like the heart of God towards the Gentiles. In his prayer he demonstrated clearly his ethnocentricity and his prejudice against the Gentiles." (Jabbour, 247)

[125] Jabbour, 55–57.

The author of *Distinctly Welcoming* places the entire focus of the book on the attitude of Christians to people of other faiths.[126] The author points to the negative attitudes of prejudices, superiority, and triumphalism and commends the attitude of respect, which includes affirming the good in the faith of others, openness and neighborliness, a spirit of humility and inquiry, reciprocity, and grace. The author does not deny the importance of learning and finding out more about the faiths of other people, but he believes that a genuine spirit of learning and a determination to listen goes a long way.[127] The Christians are called to be like Christ in their relationships.[128] The book also emphasizes that living our theology is more valuable that arguing about it.[129] In his desire to encourage Christians to interact with people of other faiths, the author puts a lot of emphasis on the fact that one needs to be conscious of who he or she is, "because the pattern of our engagement is shaped by foundational Christian concepts."[130] The underlying theme of much of this book is on the command to love one's neighbor as one's self.[131]

[126] The author writes that "if we fail to treat people of different faiths equally and with respect, we stand little or no chance of being heard as a Christian" (Sudworth, 47). He also writes that as Christians, we so often fail to see our errors and the monstrous acts of violence committed in the name of and in the pursuit of the Christian faith. "Even a cursory glance at our own history must give us pause for thought before making sweeping judgments about another faith" (Sudworth, 21). We are also encouraged to "avoid judging other groups and individuals without first judging themselves because the grace on which we are dependent is part of our memory" (Sudworth, 138).

[127] "People from another faith don't expect you to know all about their religion. They do expect to be listened to and respected." (Sudworth, 60)

[128] That means some journeying, empathizing, listening, learning… The incarnation is an indicator of what God is like: journeying, identifying, empathizing, listening" (Sudworth, 57).

[129] "Arguing simply about beliefs rarely convinces people of the validity of them. Seeing them in action makes the difference." (Sudworth, 50)

[130] Sudworth, 130.

[131] This love means that one looks "beyond the superficial labels, and do some extra work on understanding someone's relationship to their own faith", because that's exactly what I would expect of others as they reflect on my faith. "God enters into relationship

Both the book *Cross and Crescent* and the accompanying course explicitly deal with attitude.[132] The material challenges the readers/students to examine their own attitudes towards Islam and Muslims.[133] The author asserts that "in the process of sharing the good news, or perhaps even before we can be in a right frame of mind to do so, we may have to allow the Holy Spirit to do some painful things to deal with attitudes of pride in our conscious and subconscious minds."[134]

Although both are addressed by Chapman, developing personal relationships with Muslims is given priority over understanding Is-

with who we are, listening to our heart-cries, diving deep into our stories. Let's do the same for our other-faith neighbors!" (Sudworth, 151)

It means that one should not prejudge the goodwill and theology of people of other faiths, based on the behavior of some, or by the media view. "We need to find out for ourselves the nature of the other party: hopes and fears, dreams, joys and disappointments. Isn't this what we would expect for ourselves?... So let us approach people of other faiths as individuals, being open to their unique story... Let us love our neighbors as ourselves and not impose our view of 'what they think', 'what they do', without having heard and experienced these things at first-hand from this particular person" (Sudworth, 106).

[132] One of the aims of the first part of the book (pages 21–55) and the first session of the course is "to articulate the participants' questions, attitudes and concerns about Muslims and Islam." Chapter 3, entitled *Examining Our Attitudes*, deals with this matter (pages 41–55).

[133] In chapter 3 of the book the author discusses six comments about Islam, which are often made by Christians and encourages the reader that when being critical about Islam, one should use the same criteria to look at one's self and Christianity in general. He also encourages the readers to not interpret the Qur'an, but listen to how Muslims themselves interpret some controversial texts. He also refers to the principle of reciprocity. "Christians should want to be guided by the Golden Rule in which Jesus says: 'In everything, do to others what you would have them do to you, for this sums up the Law and the Prophets.' " (Mt. 7:12) (Chapman, 49) With reference to Abraham, who expected that outside his people, no one fears the Lord, but who discovered that "some people outside the covenant have a real reverence for God, and are even able to hear and respond to a direct communication from God." (Gen. 20:1–18) (52), the author notes that "our attitudes may sometimes be influenced by more than just our desire for correct doctrine" (Chapman, 51). He addresses the racial, religious and political prejudices that Christians might have towards Muslims, which might be very similar to the prejudices the Jews showed toward Samaritans at the time of Jesus (Chapman, 54).

[134] Chapman, 52.

lam. In session one of the course, the students are asked to discuss and reflect on the content of this chapter and study eight Bible passages that the author uses to help the readers think about their attitude towards Muslims.

Materials that Predominantly Address Attitude

The main goal of Steve Bell's book *Grace for Muslims* is to address the attitude problem that many Christians have towards Muslims. The author believes that the grace of God is something "that is badly needed by many western Christians who are struggling with an attitude problem towards Muslims."[135] The author's desire is to enable Christians to move from prejudice to understanding, from fear to friendship, and from fear of Muslims to faith for them. The main attitude that is encouraged is a grace response to Muslims.[136] The author refers to grace as the place "where a Muslims and a Christian can stand together"[137] and gives eleven reasons why it is appropriate for a Christian to extend grace towards a Muslim.[138]

135 Chapman, 6.

136 By grace-response the author means "a willingness to alter the default mechanism in our brains which causes us to fear the unfamiliar in another person; being prepared to give others the benefit of the doubt and make an effort to find out why they behave as they do. A grace response is willing to include the other person within the scope of God's love and the Great Commission of Jesus Christ rather than imagining there is an exclusion clause which puts them beyond our concern (1). He realize that it is not easy to urge a grace response when people feel threatened," However the grace response is a stance that Jesus Christ demanded of his followers in Matt. 5:44 and which Paul urged in Rom. 12: 14–21) (Bell, Grace, 55).

He realizes that responding with grace is a high ideal, "however, it is clear: grace towards the Muslim is possible. This is because it is under-girded by the biblical certainty that the divine plan will win out" (Bell, Grace, 57, 58).

137 Steve Bell, *Grace*, 30.

138 Steve Bell, *Grace*, 140–160.

The objective of Steve Bell in his manual *Friendship First* is not so much to inform, but to affect the reader.[139] The main thrust is to help Christians overcome attitudinal and emotional barriers that create a lack of understanding for Islam and Muslims and hinder Christians from building friendships with Muslims and using opportunities to share the Good News of Jesus Christ with them.[140] Bell's manual is aimed at affecting the attitude and emotions of the students and provide them with accurate information.[141] While it does not deny the dark side of political Islam, it explicitly gives reasons why it does not share the fear of some Christian leaders that the West will become Islamic. In addition, the manual challenges the reader to "keep the words *Islam* and *Muslim* in separate mental compartments and to resist being suspicious of 'ordinary?' Muslims." Based on the biblical command to love the stranger in their midst, the manual wants to move the student from an attitude of "resentment" to one of "tolerance" and then "love". The main attitude that is promoted is "grace", while attitudes that are discouraged are "suspicion", "fear", "resentment" and "superiority."[142]

[139] Throughout the material our attitude is discussed, e. g. in chapter 2, the material contains a list of Bible passages that deals with attitudes towards others and encourages the student to think 'Christianly' about Muslims (17). The author states that the manual is about an A, E, I, O, U, of friendship with Muslims: Attitude, Emotions, Information, Opportunities and Understanding. (Bell, Friendship, 11,12).

[140] The author believes that main barriers against friendship with Muslims are attitudinal and emotional barriers. "These barriers stop us coming out onto the bridge of friendship" (Bell, Friendship, 24). These barriers persist "partly because we are starved of information about each other. We therefore avoid opportunities. Together all this creates the lack of understanding…" (Bell, *Friendship*, 29)

[141] Because the author believes that "when we have faced our attitude and emotions we are in a better position to receive accurate information about Muslims." (Bell, *Friendship*, 11)

[142] Ibid.

Summary of the Analysis of Books/Courses[143]

Table 1: Summary of the Analysis of Books/Courses

Book/course	Open and Closed	Dialogue and Apologetics	Knowledge and Attitude
Grace for Muslims	6	8	14
Cross and Crescent	15	14	13
The Call of the Minaret	11	6	9
The Crescent through the eyes of the Cross	9	7	11
Ask your Muslim Friend	8	12	8
Muslims and Christians at the Table	4	10	5
Faith to Faith	14	5	7
Islam: the Challenge to the Church	3	2	2
Distinctly Welcoming	10	15	12
Friendship First	12	9	15
Developing a Heart for Muslims	5	1	4
Engaging with Islam	1	3	1
Carey Course in Christian-Muslim Relations	7	11	6
Life Challenge Materials	2	4	3
Encountering the World of Islam	13	13	10

Of the sixteen books and courses[144] analyzed, three have a predominantly closed view on Islam; one has a somewhat closed view; and one has mostly an open view, but with pockets of a closed view. These materials focus mostly on ideal, original, or standard Islam and hardly pay attention to the way Islam is practiced in the real lives of Muslims.

Also these materials tend to compare the worst in Islam with the best of Christianity. They paint a predominantly negative picture

143 The lower the number, the more closed view of Islam, the more against dialogue and the more emphasis on knowledge. The higher the number, the more open view of Islam, the more positive about dialogue, the more emphasis on attitude.

144 Because the book *Cross and Crescent: Responding to the Challenge of Islam* has been taken together with the course *Cross and Crescent*, one finds only fifteen entries in the overview above.

of Islam and fail to differentiate differences among Muslims and make general stereotypical statements.

Of the five materials with a closed view of Islam, two are also silent or ambivalent about meeting with Muslims on a personal basis; two are predominantly apologetic and one is polemical. These materials focus mostly on theological issues and usually are negative about dialogue with Muslims.

The other eleven books and courses have a predominantly open view of Islam, but express this attitude differently; two look at Islam in a critical but respectful way; four look for the person behind the Muslim; five emphasize a willingness to look for positive aspects within Islam.

These materials encourage Christians to feel at ease in the presence of Muslims and to look at them from a human perspective and not just from a theological perspective. Five books/courses speak about friendship with Muslims and stimulate the reader to stand in the Muslim's shoes, but do not explicitly encourage the student to meet with Muslims as part of the course/book. Three books/courses explicitly encourage Christians to meet with Muslims and are positive about an apologetic approach and are also open to dialogue. Two books/courses encourage the reader/student to meet Muslims and favor dialogue above apologetic. One book balances witness with dialogue.

When one looks at the materials through the "knowledge and attitude" lens, one finds that the materials with a predominantly closed view of Islam place more emphasis on providing information about Islam than addressing the attitude of Christians toward Islam. One book provides the information about Islam in a biased way, and the information of four books/courses can lead to a growing attitude of fear towards Islam. Five books/courses put more emphasis on information than on attitude and present the information on Islam in a respectful way. Four materials put more emphasis on attitude than on information, and two books/courses predominantly address the attitude and hardly touch on information.

Conclusion

The materials that seem to be most helpful in helping Christians deal with their attitude towards Islam and encourage them to share their lives with them would be those that (1) explicitly address the negative attitude of Christians towards Islam and Muslims and help them deal with it in light of Scripture, while not ignoring the need to provide them with accurate information about Islam; (2) look at the person behind the Muslims and consider them not just in a theological way, but as a fellow religious human being with fears and needs; (3) explicitly encourage Christians to build relationships with Muslims; and (4) have an open view of Islam, with a willingness to acknowledge the positive aspects of Islam and a willingness to look critically at one's own Christian practice, so as to not compare Islam's reality with Christianity's ideals, and be willing to include Islamic sources in their material.

Of the materials analyzed *Cross and Crescent* (both the book and the course), *Distinctly Welcoming*, *Encountering the World of Islam* and *Friendship First* seem to accomplish the purpose mentioned above.

I pointed out in chapter two that the attitude which Christians need to overcome is fear and the attitude Christians need to adopt is grace. This matter is dealt with to some extent in the four materials mentioned above. However, if one believes that (1) fear, prejudice, and suspicion are key attitudes for Christians to address in light of Islam; (2) only the Holy Spirit enables Christians to deal with fear in general and fear of Islam/Muslims in particular, it might be necessary to look at this fear more explicitly and in more detail in light of Scripture. Also, if one believes that (1) the most appropriate attitude of Christians towards Muslims and Islam in accordance with the example of their Lord and Savior Jesus Christ is one of embracing and showing grace to those they dislike, and (2) that only the Holy Spirit can replace a spirit of fear with that of grace and love in the midst of hostility, it is important that one has a more detailed look at grace from a biblical perspective. Christians must understand that they are not only recipients of grace, but are also called to be channels of that grace towards others in general. In the context of one's relationship with Muslims, a grace attitude to Muslims is of particular importance.

What is needed is a tool that is easily accessible for ordinary Christians. A tool is needed that does not require a lot of reading or studying and is something that can be used in small groups in homes of believers, where there is an opportunity to interact and can be used for a limited period of time. Also, a tool is needed that provides Christians with the opportunity to actually meet and interact with Muslims. None of the materials mentioned above meet all those criteria.

Two of the materials (*Friendship First* and *Cross and Crescent*) are books, which makes them less suitable for the purposes mentioned above. Although *Distinctly Welcoming* is a book, it could be used in small groups because each chapter includes questions to help the reader process the information read; nevertheless the book does not focus on Muslims in particular. *Encountering the World of Islam* is a good course, but with its six hundred- page text book and twelve lessons, it is too heavy as an introductory course.

The course that is written accompanying the book *Cross and Crescent* emphasizes relating to Muslims. It addresses the Christian's attitude toward Muslims and Islam; it provides information about Islam and gives some tools as to how to share the Gospel with Muslims with all the material to be covered in five sessions of 1.5 hours each, but looking at the content covered, this ideal seems hard to do.[145] Visiting a mosque is discussed and encouraged in the first session of the course, but the actual visit has to be done outside the five lessons.

[145] The workbook itself admits this, because one reads on page 1: "this workbook contains more material than can be covered in the five sessions of this course."

Although this course comes closest to meeting the criteria mentioned above, it still is not a short course that explicitly deals with the attitude of Christians toward Muslims nor is it a course that starts with addressing attitude and gradually moves toward information and building relationships. In the next chapter, I present a course, entitled Sharing Lives, which seems to meet all the criteria previously discussed.

The content and format of the course Sharing Lives has not only been shaped by the thoughts presented in this dissertation, but also is guided by the following four concepts gleaned from the material that has been analyzed in this chapter: (1) the importance of incarnational witness as found in *Encountering the World of Islam*; (2) the idea of a grace response to Muslims and the thought that the main barriers against friendship with Muslims are attitudinal and emotional barriers as discussed in *Friendship First*; (3) to take seriously the command to "love your neighbor as yourself," as argued in the book *Distinctly Welcoming*, which includes approaching Muslims as individuals and not imposing on them one's view of "what they think" and "what they do," without having heard and experienced these things first-hand from this particular person; (4) the model of genuine meeting and dialogue that is given for the relationship between a Christian and a Muslim based on Luke's description of Jesus in the temple at the age of twelve (Luke 2:45, 46), and which consists of (1) sitting among them; (2) listening; (3) asking questions; (4) understanding; (5) offering answers, which are found in the book and course *Cross and Crescent*.

Chapter Four
Sharing Lives: A Course for Christians

Having concluded that the main obstacle for Christians to share their lives and their faith with Muslims is fear, suspicion, and prejudice, I have argued that most of the current books and courses that were reviewed only briefly look at the attitude of Christians toward Islam and Muslims and focus primarily on information explaining the various aspects of Islam. The main exceptions are the materials written by Steve Bell, which give a higher priority to dealing with attitude than with providing information.[1] These materials also encourage an attitude of grace, which is the attitude that is recommended throughout this dissertation.

In the previous chapter, I have concluded that although the researched materials contain elements that are useful to help Christians overcome their fear of Islam and Muslims and encourage them to share their lives with Muslims, none of the materials include all of what is needed in a format that can be offered by way of a course to ordinary Christians in churches across Europe to help them to share their lives with Muslims.

Therefore, I suggested that a new course be developed, entitled Sharing Lives, based on the findings of this dissertation and influenced by some of the key concepts of the best materials analyzed.

Name

The course is given the name Sharing Lives because the projected main outcome is that people share not just the Gospel with Muslims, but their lives as well. This thought has been taken from 1 Thess. 2:8: "We loved you so much that we were delighted to

[1] Bell states that "when we have faced our attitude and emotions we are in a better position to receive accurate information about Muslims." (Bell, Friendship, 11).

share with you not only the gospel but our lives as well, because you had become so dear to us." In the introduction of this dissertation I have looked at the background of this verse.

Objective

The main objective of the course is to help people change their attitude towards Islam and Muslims from one of fear to one of grace and to encourage them to develop meaningful relationships with Muslims in their neighborhood in order to share their lives and the Gospel of Jesus Christ with them.

Outcome

The course intends to encourage Christians to share their lives with Muslims in five steps. Each step is addressed in one lesson. The first step is to look at one of the main obstacles of sharing one's life with a Muslim, namely fear. The second step is to draw attention to one of the main ingredients needed in sharing one's life with a Muslim, namely an attitude of grace. The third step is to understand Muslims and their faith and culture. The fourth step is to actually interact with Muslims and hear how they express their faith in daily life as well as their dreams and fears. The fifth and final step is achieved by explaining what it means to be an incarnational witness to one's Muslim friend.

Duration and Group Size

The course consists of five sessions of 1.5 hours each and has been designed to be given during five consecutive weeks. The ideal size of the group is between five and ten people. Such size makes interaction with each other and Muslims easier and makes it possible for the course to be given in someone's home, which might be more attractive to potential students.

Materials

The students will be given written notes of most lessons. The teaching will be supported by PowerPoint presentations and DVDs.

Lessons[2]

Lesson 1: Understanding our Fear of Islam
Lesson 2: Developing a Grace Response to Muslims
Lesson 3: Understanding Muslims
Lesson 4: Meeting with Muslims
Lesson 5: Building Relationships that Last

The Content

Lesson 1: Understanding our Fear of Islam

Because the main attitudes to overcome are fear, prejudice, and suspicion, the first lesson is called Understanding our Fear of Islam and addresses the fear of Islam and Muslims and brings this attitude out into the open. Most likely many of the reasons for fear of Islam and Muslims, which are listed in chapter 2 of this dissertation, will be mentioned during this lesson. Because most of the facts that are used to justify one's fear of Islam and Muslims contain elements of truth, I will not argue against them. Instead I would like to make students become aware that, as pointed out in chapter 2, when one looks beneath the attitude of fear, one might discover that it probably has more to do with one's fallen human nature than with the words or deeds of Muslims.

After looking at God's call to Jonah and his disobedience to share his life with his enemies in Nineveh (which partly might have been caused by fear) and drawing some parallels to one's attitude to Muslims, the students are asked to express and articulate their

[2] For a more detailed outline of the lessons, see Appendix C.

view of Islam and Muslims by writing on a piece of paper some words, images, thoughts, pictures that come to mind when thinking of Islam and Muslims. They are then asked to finish the sentences: When it comes to Islam, I fear...; when it comes to Islam, I suspect that...; when it comes to Islam, I find it unfair that...

The results will be discussed in the group without criticizing what is being said, because the main objective is to make the students more aware of their attitudes toward Islam.

Then the group will look at one section of a DVD, entitled *Inside Islam.*[3] This part of the DVD is focused on fundamentalist and extreme Muslims who commit atrocities in different parts of the world and how other Muslims respond to these atrocities. The reason to show this video is to point out that, while there are extremists that use Islam to commit violence, there is another side to Islam. As I argued in chapter 2 one of the features of Islamophobia is a closed view of Islam. By having students look at this DVD, I would like to help them develop a more open view of Islam.

After viewing the DVD, the students will look at fear in the light of Scripture. Particular attention is drawn to Isaiah 40–54. In this passage the people of God are in a difficult situation. They fear losing their identity as the people of God because it seems that the powers and gods around them are stronger than the God of Israel and that although their past was great, their future is dark. During this time when the people of God were fearful, doubtful, and uncertain about their survival and future, God sent the prophet Isaiah to the people with a message of comfort and promise and a reminder to who God is, saying: "Say to those with fearful hearts, "Be strong, do not fear; your God will come, he will come with vengeance; with divine retribution he will come to save you" (Is. 35:4). God does so with the frequent admonition to "fear not" and gives

[3] *Inside Islam*, DVD, dir. Mark Hufnail, 100. (A&E Home Video, 2003). A documentary that provides an introduction to Islam. Topics include Islam's connections with Judaism and Christianity, the life of Muhammad, the Five Pillars of Islam, the history of Islam, women in Islam, European colonialism, Islamism, the Nation of Islam, and jihad.

his people a rationale for doing so. In Isaiah 40–54 the prophet has a lot to say about fear. These chapters are therefore appropriate for believers in our times to meditate on when addressing their fears of militant Islam and in a context in which the church in Europe fears its future and its identity and points to the Islamization of the continent.

Also, in this part of the Bible one finds four "Servant Songs" (42:1–9; 49:1–6, 50:4–9, 52:13–53:12). The great work of the Lord on behalf of Israel, and on behalf of the entire world, is accomplished through the work of this figure. The character and ministry of this Servant is fulfilled by Jesus. It is not without significance that three of the four Servant Songs, speak of suffering. Particularly Isaiah 53 refers to the self-giving love of the Servant, as exemplified in the cross, which I have pointed out in chapter two of this dissertation is the model for one's relationship with Muslims. Therefore, this lesson points out that God's purposes for his servants involves the cross, no matter what.

The homework students are given after this first lesson is prayer. The reason is that rational arguments (e. g. that Islam is not just extremists, or that there are some changes taking place in Islam, or that Islam is not as black as some say it is) by themselves do not change people's attitudes. What is needed is a work of God in their hearts. Therefore, the students are asked to bring the papers on which they have written their views of Islam into the presence of the Lord during the next seven days. It is expected that when people bring their fears honestly, sincerely and seriously into the presence of the Lord and are willing to listen to him (through his Word), the Holy Spirit can deal with their hearts.

As a help and guideline for their prayers, they will be asked to meditate on seven Psalms. The book of Psalms gives a good insight in the inner lives of David and other believers. When one reads the Psalms it becomes clear that believers of the past were people like modern believers, with their fears and anxieties. The Psalmists did not allow their lives be dominated by fear, but brought their fears before the Lord in prayer, where it disappeared in the light of God's presence. The students are asked to read through one Psalm during each of the following seven days: Day 1: Psalm 27; Day 2: Psalm 55; Day 3: Psalm 56; Day 4: Psalm 69; Day 5: Psalm 91; Day 6: Psalm 109; Day 7: Psalm 137.

These Psalms are chosen because each of them deals with an aspect of fear or threat and gives insight as to how the Psalmist brings his fear, anger, and anxiety into the presence of God. Included are Psalms that call for the Divine wrath upon one's enemies (e.g. 109, 137), which sometimes puzzle Christians. These Psalms are included to help the students deal with possible anger in their lives regarding some aspect of Islam.

Lesson 2: Developing a Grace Response to Muslims

It is expected that when students continue to bring their fear of Islam into the presence of God, there will come opportunity to develop another attitude toward Islam and Muslims, namely one of grace. This attitude will be the main subject of lesson 2, which is called Developing a Grace Response to Muslims.[4]

After discussing how the students have experienced the homework (prayer) of the past week, the lesson continues to look at an aspect of the life of Jonah. It is pointed out how Jonah as a disobedient servant of God experienced God's saving grace, but was reluctant to be a channel of that same grace to the people of Nineveh, whom he disliked.

In order to help students understand and appreciate the depth and richness of the biblical concept of grace, this lesson includes a Bible study on grace, explaining that grace is part of who God is throughout the Bible and that grace is related to all main doctrines in the Bible. Also, the students will look at how the Bible encour-

[4] The term *grace response* and the definition of it, has been taken from the book *Grace for Muslims*, by Steve Bell.

ages us to be dispensers of God's grace and how this encouragement is worked out in our lives, attitudes and words.

The students will look at another section of *Inside Islam*, which explains how Muslims glorify their history and point to the golden age of Islam, including the times when Islam ruled in Spain. The reason for showing this part of the DVD is to help students understand Islam through the eyes of Muslims, which is part of an attitude of grace. After watching the DVD, the students will specifically learn about what it means to develop a culture of embrace, an attitude of grace, and a behavior modeled on the cross towards Islam and Muslims. It is pointed out that this culture, attitude and behavior is characterized by: (1) applying the golden rule, (2) loving one's Muslim neighbor as one loves oneself; (3) not giving false testimony about one's Muslim neighbor; (4) a willingness to recognize the positive aspects of Islam; (5) an ability to view Muslims as human beings, and (6) to recognize God's promises to the descendants of Ishmael in the Bible (Gen. 17:20).

The homework to be taken from the second lesson is the prayer of Saint Francis of Assisi. Students are asked to pray this prayer with Muslims in mind every day for the next week. This prayer is chosen because Saint Francis is a good example of a Christian who extended grace to Muslims in a time (during the Crusades) when many fellow Europeans distrusted and feared Muslims.[5]

Lesson 3: Understanding Muslims

After having faced their attitude and emotions towards Islam and Muslims, students are expected to be in a better position to receive accurate information about Islam and Muslims. Therefore, this third lesson is called Understanding Muslims.

[5] In his book *Grace for Muslims?* Steve Bell describes Saint Francis as "a Christian who balanced political realism with a gracious attitude towards Muslims."(5). He also refers to this prayer and writes that "The answer to this prayer can only be possible through the grace of God." (6)

The lesson starts with an opportunity for feedback on the homework given from previous lesson. They will watch another part of the DVD *Inside Islam*, including the topics that look at the beginning of Islam, the life of Muhammad, the *Qur'an*, and the link with Christianity through Abraham and Ishmael.

Having looked at Jonah from a biblical perspective in the previous two lessons, this lesson will look at him from an Islamic point of view. The students will read some verses from the *Qur'an* that speak of Jonah and compare what the *Qur'an* says about him with the biblical references. Also, the relevance of Jonah (particularly his prayer) in the life of contemporary Muslims is explained.

Then the students are taken through the following aspects of Islam: (1) origins of Islam; (2) the person of Muhammad; (3) the expansion of Islam; (4) what Muslims believe (particularly zooming in on the three most important doctrines: the unity of God, the importance of prophet hood, and life after death); (5) the five pillars of Islam; (6) authority in Islam (*Qur'an*, *Sunnah*, law schools); (7) branches and movements within Islam; (8) Islamic culture and customs and (9) how Muslims view Christians.

After a time of interaction and discussion, the lesson finishes with a brief video clip in which a Muslim sings about the beauty of Islam. The reason for showing this clip is to have the students understand that, for many Muslims, Islam is an attractive religion that receives their full devotion, without leading to aggression or violence and to develop in them a growing open view of Islam.

The homework given is to prepare next lesson, which is a meeting with Muslims. The students are asked to list some specific questions they would like to ask the Muslims they will be meeting. As a help, they are given a handout with thirty six possible questions.[6]

[6] Some of these questions are taken from the book *Ask your Muslim Friend*, by Andreas Maurer.

Lesson 4: Meeting with Muslims

Having prepared the student's attitudes and taught them some basic information about Islam, it is time that the students meet and interact with Muslims. This lesson is called Meeting with Muslims. The meeting can take place in a mosque, an Islamic center, in a Muslim's home, or having Muslims visit the location where the course takes place.

Prior to the visit the students are given the homework to do afterwards. They are asked to reflect on what was most prominent and what was most appreciated about the faith of the Muslims they met. They are also asked to read through Acts 10 and reflect on the relationship between Cornelius and Peter. Cornelius is called a god-fearing person, which meant that he was sympathetic towards Judaism. He was devout, gave alms, and prayed regularly. The student is asked to compare the Muslims they have met with what the Bible says about Cornelius, giving emphasis on how they are similar and how they are different. Also they are asked to reflect on the prayers of Muslims. Assuming that praying has been a subject during the conversation with Muslims, the students are asked to reflect on the prayers of Muslims in light of Cornelius' prayer with questions such as: do you think that God answers their prayers? What do you think happens when they pray?[7]

Lesson 5: Building Relationships that Last

Because one of the main goals of the course is to encourage people to become a friend of a Muslims, the last session focuses on what it means to be a relational witness to Muslims. This lesson is entitled Building Relationships that Last.

After feedback on last week's homework, the students will learn about the importance of incarnational or relational witness,[8]

[7] These thoughts and questions are taken from the book *Distinctly Welcoming*, by Richard Sudworth.

[8] This concept, and its description, has been borrowed from the course *Encountering the World of Islam.*

which is also called friendship evangelism. It is pointed out that proclamation and incarnation needs to be integrated and that one's theology is seen in one's behavior. The students are given some "do's and don'ts" in relationship with Muslims (such as: beware of differences between sexes, use your Bible with respect, and be prepared to speak about anything). Some guidelines are given when sharing the Gospel with Muslims (such as, do not attack Islam; do not force the issue; do all you can to remove misunderstandings; use personal testimony; and walk the talk).

The students are then presented with a model for meeting and dialogue, based on Luke 2: 46, 47, where Jesus as a twelve year old boy is in the temple. The elements of this model are sitting among them; listening, asking questions, understanding, and answers.[9] The students are given several practical ways to connect naturally with Muslims: sports, participating in community projects, running homework clubs for children; using Muslim business services etc and also given suggestions as to how to develop natural relationships with Muslims.

The homework given after this final lesson involves asking the students to ask God to guide each one of them personally to one Muslim whom he wants them to develop a relationship with for his glory.

This lesson finishes with a DVD which presents a dramatized story of the life of Khalil, a fundamentalist Muslim who came to faith in Jesus Christ.[10] The reason this DVD is shown at the end is to encourage the students that God is at work among Muslims, and he is able to bring some that cause fear among Christians to

[9] This model is taken Colin Chapman's book *Cross and Crescent.*

[10] *More than Dreams* 187. (Vision Video, 2007). *More than Dreams,* which contains five true-life stories of former Muslims who now know Jesus as their Savior. The stories were selected from Egypt, Iran, Turkey, Nigeria, and Indonesia. More Than Dreams recreated each of these stories, producing each in its original language, in a docu-drama format. The movies include a ministry segment explaining what it means to follow Christ and leading viewers in the salvation prayer. See: http://www.morethandreams.org/index.html

himself, using his word and the lives of his people who were willing to share their lives with Muslims.

For Further Study

Because in a brief introductory course such as Sharing Lives not everything can be said, the students are given a list of books and DVD's and addresses of organizations that can help them study Islam further and provide them with more in-depth information on how to share the Gospel with Muslims in relevant ways.

Chapter Five
Testing and Evaluating Course Sharing Lives

In order to learn whether the course Sharing Lives does develop a changed attitude of the participants toward Islam and Muslims, a desire to build relationships with Muslims, and a desire to share their lives and the Gospel with their Muslim friends, the course was run as a pilot in three different places in the Netherlands for three different groups.[1] This chapter gives an overview of the selection of the groups, a description of the groups and how the course was conducted with each group, the attitude of the group prior to taking the course, the feedback of the students, and a reflection of the results and feedback.

Selecting the Groups to Pilot the Course

An email was send to about eighty people to ask whether they were interested in having the course run as a pilot in their church, organization, or school. From the responses that came back, a decision was made to run the course as a pilot in three groups, during the months October through December 2008, namely at a) Amsterdam Bible Academy, Amsterdam; b) a an evangelical church in Soest; and c) a Bible school in Zeist.

[1] Although in light of the European scope of this research, it would have been more advantageous to run pilots in several European countries, but this was not possible within the time constraints of this research. I have used parts of the course during a missions' conference in Belgium in September 2008 and during an European leaders meeting of Operation Mobilization in Germany in November 2008.

Description of the Groups

Amsterdam Bible Academy, Amsterdam

The Amsterdam Bible Academy (ABA) is designed to enhance the spiritual growth of African Christians in and around Amsterdam and to prepare them for ministry. Its core curriculum is the International Correspondence Institute Christian Service series. ABA is affiliated with Global University, Springfield, Missouri, in the United States and offers courses at two levels: Christian service level (CS) and Bachelor's Degree in Ministries and Theology. Both courses are offered on Saturdays when students attend classes from 9:00–14:30h.

The course Sharing Lives was offered to all students as an option to be taken after the last class, on five consecutive Saturdays from 14:30–16:00h. Of the total enrollment of twenty-five students, sixteen signed up to take the course Sharing Lives, and most attended all the classes. All of the students were Christians from African background (particularly Ghana and Nigeria), who live in the Netherlands and are active members or leaders of African churches in Amsterdam and elsewhere. Most students were between thirty to fifty years old and predominantly male. Most of the students had limited previous contact with Muslims in the Netherlands. The course was given in English.

Evangelical Church Soest

The second pilot took place with seven members of an evangelical church in Soest. Most of the participants knew each other from church, although they had never met in this context. Most of the participants already had previous contact with Muslims

as colleagues, neighbors or during evangelistic outreaches. Their ages varied between twenty-four and sixty-five, and the group consisted of two women and five men. The course took place on Monday evenings from 20:00–21:30h in the home of one of the participants. Although the PowerPoint and the DVD presentations were in Dutch, most of the written notes were in English.

Bible School De Wittenberg, Zeist

The third pilot took place at De Wittenberg, a Christian school in Zeist that emphasizes development of personal faith, being a disciple of Jesus Christ, and discovering one's place in society. The school offers several one-year programs and has about sixty students each year. The students choose this school after having completed their university education or after having had a job for several years. These students live together on campus, and after finishing the one year program, many students continue to serve God full-time in a church or Christian organization, both in the Netherlands and abroad.

The course Sharing Lives was offered as part of the curriculum to seven students of the program Missionary Work, four of whom are preparing for missionary work abroad and three for missionary work in the Netherlands. The students varied from twenty-one to forty-four years of age. The course took place during regular school hours and was conducted in Dutch. Because the course was part of the regular curriculum of the school's program, it was requested that the total number of hours needed to attend the classes and do the homework be set at twenty-eight hours. The course Sharing Lives would normally take about nine hours. Therefore, extra homework assignments were added when conducting the course at the Bible school.[2]

[2] Such as: reading several chapters of the book *Cross and Crescent: responding to the Challenge of Islam* by Colin Chapman, which the students had to buy at the beginning of the school year and also to write a profile of the Muslim community in their town/city and how their church could reach them with the Gospel.

The Attitude of the Participants Prior to Taking the Course

Before the course began, all participants were asked to comment on forty-four statements about Muslims and Islam.[3]

Some of the statements reflect negative thinking towards Islam and Muslims regarding their relationship with the West.[4] Others pertain to common prejudices toward Islam or Muslims.[5] Still other statements reflect a closed view of Islam, which as was pointed out earlier, is one of the characteristics of *Islamophobia*.[6] For each of the statements, the participants could choose one of the following boxes: strongly agree, agree, neutral, disagree, or strongly disagree. The objective of this exercise was to learn more about the attitude and perspective of the participants relative Islam and Muslims, prior to taking the course. In order to find out whether there is a significant difference between the attitude of those who participated in the course and others from their church/school, the same questionnaires were also handed out to non-participants of the course.

[3] See Appendix D for a list of these statements. Most of the statements were taken from the questionnaire of the Culture, Media and Communication Department of the University of Surrey. See http://latifkhan.co.uk/questionare/questionarenew.htm. Some of their statements were left out and others were added, because it was felt these were more appropriate to the Dutch context. The questionnaires were sent to the contact person of the church/group/school and were handed out by them to those who would participate in the course. The (anonymous) questionnaires were handed in at the beginning of the first lesson and were not commented on at all during the course.

[4] "Islam is a threat to our civilization" or "Islam is opposed to the western way of life" or "Islam is the biggest threat to our national identity" or "Muslims are destroying our culture".

[5] "Islam's desire is to take over our country" or "Most Muslim immigrants don't want to integrate in Europe" or "Muslims will destroy our democratic system, if they could" or "Muslims do not show their real face until they are a majority" or "Geert Wilders is right about the growing Islamization of the Netherlands and Europe"

[6] "Islam is a religion of aggression and violence," "Muslims can't be trusted," or "The Qur'an encourages violence against Christians."

In total, the questionnaire was filled out by forty-seven people, twenty-six of whom have taken the course *Sharing Lives*.[7]

One must be careful not to draw firm conclusions from the responses because people had no opportunity to explain why they responded the way they did, and one does not know whether their responses would be different in another context. With this precaution in mind, one nevertheless can generally identify the following outcomes:

A Reluctant Acceptance of Islam in Our Society

Overall the respondents seem to reluctantly accept the idea that Islam has a place in our society. Eighty percent believe Muslims have the right to practice their religion in the Netherlands and 65 percent agree that Muslims have the right to build mosques in the Netherlands, and just more than half (54 percent) do not mind having Muslims in our local or national governments. Although about the same number (52 percent) would not mind if the government restricts the entry of Muslims into the Netherlands, and a significant minority (30 percent) believe that religious activities of Muslims should be restricted in the Netherlands. This ambivalent attitude among the respondents becomes clear in that 45 percent of those that agree that Islam is and should be part of our multicultural society are the same as those that disagree.

[7] Those who filled out the questionnaire: ABA: fourteen participants Sharing Lives; seven others from the same church/background; Wittenberg: five participants; five non-participants, who have had another course in Islam at the school; five non-participants, who have not had another course in Islam at the school; Soest: seven participants; four non-participants. In this latter town, twenty-one non-participants were send a questionnaire by e-mail; seven responded, four filled in the questionnaire and three wrote they didn't want to fill out the questionnaire because they felt they didn't know enough about Islam or because they felt the statements were too general. For details of the results of the questionnaire, see Appendix E.

The Relationship of Islam with the West is Considered a Troublesome One

This reluctance to accept Islam as part of one's society might be caused by the overall assumption that the relationship of Islam with the West is a troublesome one.

Although 80 percent of the respondents believe that religious Muslims can be good and loyal citizens of the Netherlands, a significant number (43 percent) believe that most Muslim immigrants do not want to integrate in Europe. Seventy percent believe that Islam is opposite to the western way of life and more than half (51 percent) do not believe that Islam is tolerant to other cultures. At the same time, 27 percent believe that Muslim civilization is as good and as high a level as western civilization.

Islam is Considered a Minor Threat to Our Identity and Culture, a More Important Threat to Our Civilization and Values, and a Major Threat to Our Freedom

Most respondents do not consider Islam the biggest threat to the Dutch national identity[8] and only 19 percent believe that Muslims are destroying Dutch culture. A bigger group, namely 39 percent believe, that Muslims will destroy Western democratic system, if they could,[9] and almost half (47 percent) consider Islam a threat to Western civilization.[10] A majority of all respondents (55 percent) believe that the growth of the number of Muslims is dangerous for the freedom of Christians.

[8] An exception is the African respondents. Of the 26 percent who consider Islam the biggest threat to Dutch national identity, 83 per cent are Africans.

[9] Seventy one percent of the African participants believe that Muslims will destroy Western democratic system, if they could.

[10] All the students of the Bible school in Zeist, who have had a course in Islam, but who did not take the Sharing Lives course, consider Islam a threat to Western civilization, but 80 percent of their fellow students who haven't done a course in Islam disagree.

Islam is Associated with Violence

This feeling of danger regarding the future of Christians as the number of Muslims continues to grow in Europe might be based on the fact that some people associate Islam with violence. Most respondents (68 percent), however, do not believe that Muslim extremists (Taliban, Al Qaeda) represent true Islam. A majority (63 percent) do not believe that typical Muslims are violent, aggressive, and fanatical and consider most Muslims to be non-violent and peaceful. At the same time, more respondents (30 percent) see Islam as a religion of aggression and violence than those that do not (28 percent) and 70 percent agree with or were not willing to explicitly disagree with the statement that "it is because of Islam that there are troubles in Israel." A majority (61 percent) does not consider Islam to be a religion of peace and 51 percent believe Islam encourages violence against non-Muslims. The reason that some people associate Islam with violence might well be found in the teachings of the *Qur'an* and the example of Muhammad. A minority of the respondents (31 percent) believe that the *Qur'an* encourages terrorism, almost half (47 percent) believe it encourages violence against Christians, and 43 percent state that "because Muhammad was a warlord, fighting is part of what Islam is."

The Intentions of Muslims are Questioned and Their Motives Suspected

This apparent tension between the teaching of Islam, which many consider stimulating violence, and the perception that Muslims for most part are non-violent and peaceful may explain why a significant number of respondents question the intentions of Muslims and suspect their motives. A minority (29 percent) of the respondents wholeheartedly wants to give Muslims the benefit of the doubt, and 70 percent do not explicitly disagree with the statement that "Muslims do not show their real face until they are a majority," and a significant number of respondents (43 percent) are not willing to trust Muslims. For a significant minority of respondents (36 percent), this lack of trust might be caused by the fact that they think Jihad for Muslims means to subjugate foreign lands and people. Less than half (41 percent) are willing to state that they do not believe that it is Islam's desire to take over the Netherlands country, and this expectation might explain why 60 percent of the respondents agree with the right wing Member of Parliament Geert Wilders, who time and again warns against the growing Islamization of the Netherlands and Europe. Wilders, head of the Freedom Party, in an interview with the Dutch paper *Volkskrant* of October 6, 2006, calls the Islamization of Holland by the increasing number of Muslims the biggest problem facing the country.[11]

There Is Not a Strong Expectation of a Growing *EuroIslam*

When it comes to evaluating the influence of Islam on Europe and vice versa, more respondents expect that Islam will influence European society than that Europe will influence Islam. The expectation that Dutch society is being Islamized might be explained by the fact that only a minority (36 percent) of the respondents believes that Islam will also go through a process of secularization or that in thirty years Europe will have more liberal Muslims than conservative Muslims. This view is contrasted with a majority (68 percent) who believe that if nothing changes, there will be more Muslims than Christians in the Netherlands in forty years.

An Ambivalence Regarding Relationship between Islam and Christianity

Almost all respondents (89 percent) believe that there are areas in the society where Muslims and Christians can work together. A

[11] Militant Islam Monitor. "Geert Wilders:Head of Freedom Party calls for 'assimilation contract' and halt to non Western immigration to stop 'tsunami of Islamisation' in Holland." Militant Islam Monitor.org. http://www.militantislammonitor.org/article/id/2448 (accessed April 14, 2009).

large majority (66 percent) do not mind having Muslims as colleagues or neighbors; nevertheless, only a third (33 percent) believe that Christians can learn a lot from Islam, and a large majority (63 percent) do not want to see empty church buildings made into mosques.

Negative Attitudes Toward Islam/Muslims Are Condemned

A majority of the respondents (62 percent) condemn the negative attitude towards Muslims in others and almost half (42 percent) dislike the growing negative sentiments against Muslims in the Netherlands, which might be caused by or aggravated by the media, and almost half (44 percent) do not think the media gives a fair picture of Islam. Despite this conviction, there is still a majority of respondents (51 percent) who are not willing to state explicitly that when they talk about Muslims with their friends, their words usually are mild.

Summary

Although the majority of respondents condemned those possessing a negative attitude towards Muslims, the main attitude that surfaces when looking at the outcome of the questionnaires is a negative one: suspicion with a tendency towards fear. This fear, based upon and fed by prejudices, is strongest among the African respondents.[12]

[12] While most of the others disagreed with the statement that Islam is the biggest threat to Dutch national identity, 57 percent of the African participants agreed with this statement. Contrary to the other groups, a majority of the African believers stated that they believe Muslims will destroy the Western democratic system if they could, and 71 percent of the African participants believed that typically Muslims are violent, aggressive and fanatical. The reason might well be that many of them have grown up in Nigeria, a country where there often are clashes between Christians and Muslims.

Overall, there are no remarkable differences between those that took the course Sharing Lives and those of the same background that did not.[13]

The difference in attitude towards Islam and Muslims among the three groups that participated in the course Sharing Lives might be explained by the difference in perception of Islam and Muslims, which came out in the answers given during the first lesson to the question: "When you think of Islam, what are some of the words, images, pictures, thoughts that come to mind?"

The words mentioned by the African group were predominantly negative.[14] The other groups had a mix of positive and negative responses, and generally speaking, the Bible school students were more positive[15] than the participants from the church in Soest.[16]

During the first lesson, participants were asked to express their fears of Islam and Muslims. The following things were mentioned:

[13] Exceptions are that a majority (71 percent) of the ABA participants agreed with the statement that typically Muslims are violent, aggressive and fanatical, and that a majority (57 percent) of people of the same background disagreed with this same statement. Interestingly, all (100 percent) of the Bible School students who had not participated in the course, but had done a course on Islam previously agreed with the statement that Islam is a threat to Western civilization, but a majority of the two other groups of Bible school students disagreed. The majority (60 percent) of Bible school students who participated in the course Sharing Lives disagreed with the statement that the growth of the number of Muslims is dangerous for the freedom of Christians, while the majority (60 percent) of the two other groups of Bible school students agreed with this statement.

[14] Such as: violence; bombing; abuse of women; terrorism; not receptive for the Gospel, honor killings; fanaticism/no room for tolerance; use their power to treat others badly; they only like Muslims; culturally not flexible; their love is not real; they don't understand anything; encourage violence; bad; kind; dislike Jews; burning churches; their religion is not democratic; loyal to their faith; ready to die for their faith.

[15] Words mentioned were suppression; good deeds; 9/11; headscarf; just like me; commitment; Muhammad; minaret; Mecca; no pork; suppression of women; beating up children; viewed negatively by the media.

[16] Words mentioned were: hospitable; consistent, radical; most anti-Christian religion; generous; fear of judgment other role pattern; primitive; terrorism; knowledge of one God;women with head scarf; sheep meat; Ramadan; extremism; flag burning; kept ignorant; human, colleague, neighbor; more verbal aggression; aggression among youth/children; incited; cordial; Qur'an denies key biblical truths; heated when it comes to religion.

that we will see a clash of civilizations; that extreme right parties grow in the Netherlands; that we will see more aggression; that when Muslims take over the world, there will be no room for Christians; that the number of radical Muslims will grow; that Islam is a religion of the sword; that the influence of Muslims will grow, that Muslims will take over our country; that Muslims will persecute Christians; that Muslims will commit radical attacks. Some participants expressed the suspicion that in the near future Islam will become more influential and play a dominant role in Europe. Others said that they expect Islam will become more tolerant towards the West and that traditional values will disappear.

Some expressed their concern that Muslims often justify violence and that persecution of Christians will get worse and that Muslims perceive Christians to be unbelievers, simplistic, and immoral. Others are concerned that many Muslims are not reached with the Gospel and die without knowing the truth of Christ, but believe that when Christians do share the Gospel with Muslims, several of them will become Christians.

Evaluation of the Course

Introduction

The objective of the course Sharing Lives is to change the attitude of the participants towards Islam and Muslims and encourage them to share their lives with Muslims. I saw that the main attitude of the participants toward Muslims prior to the course was one of suspicion with a tendency to fear them. In order to discover whether the course has accomplished what it was developed to do, an evaluation is in order. In this paragraph I will particularly look at (1) the reactions of the students; (2) the pre-training questionnaire; (3) the general content of the course; (4) the notes and homework; (5) the time frame; and (6) the visit to the mosque.

The Reaction of the Students

A widely used model for evaluation training programs is Kirkpatrick's evaluation model.[17] This model identifies four levels of evaluation:

Level One- reactions of the student—what they thought and felt about the training;

Level Two- learning—the resulting increase in knowledge and capability;

Level Three- behavior—extent of behavior and capability improvement and implementation/application;

Level Four- result—the effects on the environment resulting from the trainee's performance.

Each successive level represents a more precise measure of the effectiveness of the training program, but also requires a more rigorous and time-consuming analysis.

Within the time constraints of this research exercise, the evaluation of the course Sharing Lives was predominantly level one of Kirkpatrick's model. Four months after the course was finished a limited evaluation on level three was carried out. The results are presented below.

Level One Evaluation

The primary evaluation tool was a post-training questionnaire, consisting of the following six questions:

[17] Kirkpatrick's ideas were first published in 1959, in a series of articles in the US Training and Development Journal. Alan Chapman on his website Businessball,a free ethical learning and development resource for people and organizations, writes that Donald Kirkpatrick's 1975 book Evaluating Training Programs defined his originally published ideas of 1959, thereby further increasing awareness of them, so that his theory has now become arguably the most widely used and popular model for the evaluation of training and learning. Kirkpatrick's four-level model is now considered an industry standard across the human resource and training communities. The four levels of training evaluation model was later redefined and updated in Kirkpatrick's 1998 book, called *Evaluating Training Programs: The Four Levels*. See http://www.businessballs.com/kirkpatricklearningevaluationmodel.htm

1. What have you gained the most from this course?
2. Mention at least one thing you will do as a result of attending this course.
3. In which of the three following areas has the course been most helpful to you: knowledge on Islam/Muslims; Attitude towards Islam/Muslims; Skills to relate with Muslims.
4. Think of five different people you will meet after this course. What will you tell them about it?
5. What do you think will you remember most about this course and why?
6. Can you think of three ideas (however big or small) that would help to make this a better and more valuable course?[18]

The answer to the question: What have you gained the most from this course? can be grouped into four categories: (1) the importance of relationship in witnessing about one's Christian faith to Muslims; (2) having an open view of Islam; (3) a changed attitude toward Islam/Muslims, and (4) skills for evangelizing Muslims.

The most often mentioned thing that participants will do as a result of attending this course is to establish contact with Muslims. Others mentioned they will speak differently about and relate differently to Muslims, and some mentioned they want to study more about Islam. Forty two percent of the participants stated that the course was most helpful to them because of the skills they learned, 35 percent because of the attitudes they acquired, and 20 percent because of the knowledge they gained.

From what they would say to others about the course (question four), it was clear that the most important skill they learned was related to building relationships with Muslims. The people that expressed a positive opinion of the course indicated that the course helped them in dealing with their attitude toward Muslims, parti-

[18] This questionnaire was handed out during the last lesson of the course. For more details and the specific answers to each of these questions, see Appendix F.

cularly with reference to their fear, prejudices, and unwillingness to learn from Muslims, and their judgmental and negative attitude. The participants that valued the course because of the knowledge they received, particularly referred to the background information about Islam and Muslims and the biblical perspectives relating to Muslims.

Most participants responded that the visit to the mosque will be remembered the most about the course. For some it was the first time they had visited a mosque, and others were impressed by the attitude of the people they met there and the interaction they were able to have. For several participants, the most memorable part of the course had to do with becoming aware of their attitude towards Islam and Muslims, which should not be like Jonah's attitude towards the people of Nineveh and about relating with Muslims.

The participants gave the following suggestions to make the course better and more valuable: (1) provide more information on Islam; (2) have more interaction during the lessons; (3) provide more practical tools; d) have more interaction with Muslims; and (4) include reading of the *Qur'an*.

Perhaps the following description by one of the participants, best sums up the general feedback on the course: "A small-scale course that helps you to understand the background of Islam and provides you with tools to evangelize them. A personal course that makes you think."

Level Three Evaluation

Many participants have indicated that they intend to establish contact with Muslims as a result of the course.[19] In March 2009,

[19] A little token, such as a Certificate of Completion, which was handed out to the African participants of the course Sharing Lives, might be a good reminder to them, particularly because the Certificate included the following statement: *This is to certify successful completion of the above course and the willingness to be a friend of Muslims.*

about four months after participants finished the course, I contacted two of the three groups. I met with the African students and send an email to the members of the Soest church.[20] I asked both groups whether they had been able to put their stated intentions at the end of the course into practice. All expressed an appreciation for this kind of follow-up. Among the African students one person in particular shared his experiences when sharing the Gospel with Muslims and asked for further help in relating to them. Several participants of the Soest group responded that their perception of Islam has changed,[21] and that they are approaching Muslims differently or have increased their contacts with Muslims.[22] One person started reading one of the recommended books, and someone else has made steps towards fulfilling their intention stated at the end of the course. Although I have not been able to verify whether all participants have put their intentions into action, this feedback is encouraging. There might be a need for regular follow-up and an ongoing champion to encourage people in this respect.

The Pre-training Questionnaire

One of the participants commented on the negative focus of most of the statements of the questionnaire,[23] and several of the non-participants from the church in Soest, who were sent a questionnaire, were not willing complete because of the negative overtones contained in it. There is indeed a danger of putting negatively

[20] I was not able to contact the third group, the Bible School students because they were away from school for several months due to their internship program.

[21] One person wrote that although nothing of the circumstances had changed, Muslims in his perception had gotten a more human face.

[22] One participant mentioned she in her contacts with Muslims (which haven't increased since the course) has become more aware of the importance of asking questions, listening and building relationships. Another participant mentioned that he started conversations with a Turkish baker.

[23] "I found the questionnaire at the beginning very negative; as if people were supposed to have a negative view. This was a pity and puts people in a corner."

worded statements in front of people.[24] Although each statement had been spoken literally by someone, at some time, on the questionnaire they were taken out of context. Respondents only had the five options to choose from (strongly agree, agree, neutral, disagree, strongly disagree) and could not add a rationale for their answers or justify why in some circumstances they would answer the same statement differently. This limitation of response choices might be a weakness of the questionnaire. Therefore, as mentioned before, one should be careful in drawing too strong conclusions just from the results of the questionnaire. On the other hand, the questionnaire confirms some of the findings of others as mentioned earlier in this document, and the outcomes also are confirmed by the comments made by the participants during the first lesson.

The fact that people found it difficult to agree or disagree with the statements because of the context may explain why an average of 26 percent of the statements were rated "neutral." An average of 74 percent of the people agreed or disagreed with the statements. Given the fact that about half the statements could be classified as negative towards Islam/Muslims, one would hope for a lot more "strong disagreements" than the average of 6 percent that the outcome shows. With about half of the statements being positive about Islam/Muslims, one would hope for more "strong agreements" than the average of 8 percent that I find from this questionnaire.

A questionnaire of this nature should not be the only indicator used to find out where people stand with regard to Islam. A questionnaire is not without value, if only it confronts the respondents with some of the attitudes that they thought they did not have. With all its limitations, the questionnaire does confirm my suspi-

[24] In the future, I could have one group fill out the questionnaire as it is and have the other group fill out a list with predominantly positive statements on Islam and compare whether there are any differences and to find out whether the results are caused by the negative tone of the statements.

cion of a predominantly negative attitude towards Islam and Muslims among Christians in Europe.

All the participants filled out the questionnaire prior to starting the course, without further explanation, to test their perception prior to the course. During the lessons, no reference was made to the questionnaire. If so, I might have had a better understanding of why people answered the statements the way they did, which might have given a better feedback on the content of the statements and how it comes across and whether the respondents understood the statements.

In future use of the course, the results of the questionnaire should be incorporated into the class discussions and/or as part of the evaluation of the course, e. g. ask the question: "Look at the questionnaire which you filled in before you started the course. Which statement would you rate differently if you had to fill in the questionnaire again and why?" These questions might give a clearer indication of the transformation that might have occurred in the participants.

General Content of the Lessons

The length of the lessons was 1.5 hours, except for the time in the mosque, which usually lasted two to two and a half hours. The length of the lessons was suitable and enabled the lesson to be completed easily during a midweek evening. Two groups consisted of seven participants each and one group of sixteen participants. Sixteen is a rather large group for a course of this nature. Smaller groups allow for easier interaction among one another and with Muslims. During the visits to the mosque, we met with two to five Muslims each time. Having a group of five to seven people also makes it possible to conduct the course in someone's home. The only disadvantage of this location was that we had to somewhat rearrange the living room to find an empty space on a wall to project the PowerPoint and DVD.

Using the person of Jonah as an example of someone with a wrong attitude was much appreciated because it helped participants to identify with a biblical character. Questions were raised about whether it is hermeneutically sound to apply Jonah's attitude towards Nineveh with a fear of Islam and this question needs to be looked at in more detail.

Having the outline of the course on PowerPoint was also much appreciated and it was helpful to play a short DVD presentation during each lesson. To end the last lesson with a powerful dramatized video of the conversion story of a fundamentalist Muslim from Egypt was much appreciated.

The third lesson was a lesson with basic information on Islam. This lesson was approved by an imam.[25] Perhaps in the future this lesson should be conducted by a Muslim or with one or two Muslims present.

Notes and Homework

Although the course was developed in English and the notes were written in English, only one of the three pilot courses was conducted fully in English. The other two courses were done in Dutch. The outlines and PowerPoint presentations were translated into Dutch, but most of the notes were not. The Dutch participants got the notes in English. Language had limited the impact of the course because several of the participants did not know English well enough to comfortably read the notes. From the responses it seemed that the participants did not read the notes afterwards, but the language was probably not the main cause for this negligence because it seemed that the African participants did not read the notes very well either. In the future, it is important that the notes be available to the participants in their mother tongue. Although

[25] We went over the entire content of that lesson, and afterwards he said that he really appreciated the content and the scope and said he could not have done a better job himself. In fact, he wants to have a copy of the lesson after the course is finished.

the notes were written to further clarify the lesson and to provide more biblical background (or Qur'anic background) to what was taught in the lesson, it was not followed up in a class discussion during the following lesson, nor was the homework linked to the notes. If such discussion had taken place, the impact of the course might have been greater.

The limited homework given the participants was put together to help people follow up on the lesson or prepare for the next one. Generally, people responded well to the homework given and most of the people did it reasonably well,[26] although it was hardly discussed in the following lesson.

Time Frame

The course was designed to be run during five consecutive weeks. Only for the African group did it actually happen. For the Soest group, there was a three week gap between lesson 2 and lesson 3 and the Zeist group had the first four lessons in one week, and then an almost two week gap between the fourth and the fifth lesson.

Running the course during five consecutive weeks or every two weeks seemed to be the best. Having four lessons in one week or having a three week gaps was not ideal. First of all, people need to be able to process the lessons and to reflect on its content. Regarding the first two lessons, dealing with fear and grace, one needs to come to grips with the negative attitudes in one's own heart and wrestle with the Lord about this matter in order to develop another attitude, namely one of grace. Having at least a week to do so, the participants are guided by the Psalms and the Bible studies on Isai-

[26] Particularly the homework after lesson one: reading the assigned Psalms in the light of fear or negative attitude towards Muslims was much appreciated, although some struggled to understand the hate language in some of the Psalms. Also some picked up on the homework preparing for the mosque visit by actually asking the questions that were given them as part of the notes.

ah and the concept of grace as a base for their prayers, which is important. One should not speed up this process.

The course at the Bible School in Zeist was made "heavier" with extra assignments as requested by the staff of the school, but it turned out that due to the heavy workload of the students for other classes, they were not able to meet the course deadlines. Most of the home work was done after the whole course was finished, which limits the gradual process of transformation.

At ABA the course was added to the students' normal schedule. The advantage was that people were already present on site and did not need to come specifically to attend this course. The disadvantage was that the students had had a long day and longed to go home. The extra hour and a half they had to stay for this course made the students less attentive.[27]

The Visit to the Mosque

Most students considered the visit to the mosque one of the most memorable parts of the course. Although interaction with Muslims was part of the original curriculum, initially the goal was to have participants meet with a small group of Muslims in their center or have some Muslims visit the participants during one of their classes. After discussing the objectives of such interactions (to learn more about the faith and theology of Muslims with some Muslim leaders), they suggested it would be better to meet with people in the mosque because there you find people who generally know more about Islam than the average Muslim. Preparing for the visits to the mosques took quite a bit of planning. The goal was to have people visit a mosque in the town/city where the course was conducted, so that the visit could become the beginning of a relationship. When this intention turned out to be impossible (for

[27] I therefore agree with one of the African participants who wrote in answer to the question *Can you think of three ideas that would help to make this a better and more valuable course*: "The period of the lectures should be more friendly (comfortable time)."

two groups) because it was hard to get in touch with the people in the mosque, I began to look for mosques in nearby towns. When making the appointment, the purpose of the visit was explained and a request made that we be permitted to meet several people, preferably male, female, young, and old. The Bible school students, who were according to age the youngest group, visited a mosque in Amsterdam, because this mosque is predominantly run by young Muslims. All Muslims in the mosques really took their time to interact with the students and invited us back for further visits.

The Influence of the Teacher

Some participants commented in their evaluation on the enthusiasm and experience of the teacher.[28] This comment brings up the matter of the influence of the teacher in relation to the content of the course. No assessment was done with respect to the personality and experience of the teacher or whether the teacher has had a direct bearing on the outcome of the course. Therefore, I cannot tell whether the same course taught by someone else would show a different result.

Conclusion

The course Sharing Lives was run successfully as a pilot in three locations for three very different groups of people.

The pre-training test did reveal a predominantly negative attitude among the participants, but I was careful not to draw too

[28] One response to the question: *What have you gained the most from this course?* was: "I learned a lot from Bert's enthusiasm and how he shares his faith in God." One response to the question *What do you think will you remember most about this course and why?* was: "The enthusiasm of Bert and how he shares his faith; this causes me to think and makes me enthusiastic. He speaks from experience which makes things come alive."

strong conclusions from this outcome without more interaction with the participants.

The reactions of the participants to the course were predominantly positive. From these responses, I might conclude that the two main objectives of the course, namely to help people change their predominantly negative attitude towards Islam and Muslims into a more positive one and to encourage people to build relationships with Muslims, were met to a certain extent. Regarding the first objective, 38 percent of the participants said that attitude change was the most important thing they gained from this course.[29] Regarding the second objective, 66 percent of all participants said that one thing they will do as a result of attending this course is to establish contact with Muslims.[30]

One could be satisfied with the 66 percent who want to build relationships with Muslims, but more must be done to achieve an increase in the percentage of people that change their attitude towards Muslims. Perhaps with the suggested changes and recommendations, mentioned in this chapter and the next, one could see an increase in this percentage. Care must be taken not to draw firm conclusions too soon. The 62 percent, who mentioned that the course was most helpful to them, because of skills they acquired or knowledge they gained, did not say that their attitudes were not changed in the process. To have a more accurate assessment of the course, evaluation should also include levels 2, 3 and 4 of Kirkpatrick's model. Particularly, levels 3 and 4 are important.

Level 3 measures the behavior transformation in the participant and seeks to answer the question: Are the newly acquired skills, knowledge or attitude being used in the everyday environment of the participant? This kind of evaluation requires observation over

[29] Forty percent of the students of the Soest church, 43 percent of the Bible school students, and 33 percent of the African students.

[30] Sixty percent of the students of the Soest church, 71 percent of the Bible school students and 67 percent of the African students.

a longer period of time and requires the input of others in their environment, such as their pastor or Bible study leader.

Level 4 measures the results, which in the context of this research means a friendship with Muslims. To see whether such friendship has taken place as a result of the course, one needs to hear from the participant about six months after the course.

Despite the limitations of a proper evaluation as mentioned above, it seems fair to conclude that the course Sharing Lives has proven to be a tool that can be used to help Christians overcome their fear of Islam and encourage them to share their lives with Muslims. Nevertheless, the course is still a work in progress and improvements need to be made to make it more successful. I will look at these changes in the next chapter.

Chapter Six
Summary, Conclusions and Recommendations

Summary and Conclusions

In the introduction of this dissertation, I wrote that I have been conducting seminars on how to evangelize Muslims across Europe for many years. In those seminars, I briefly touched on the matter of attitude, for example, by referring to Jonah's attitude towards the people of Nineveh; nevertheless I put a lot of emphasis on acquiring skills. Through this research project I've grown to understand the importance of dealing with attitude, and more particularly the attitude of fear. In education, often three domains of learning are identified: skill, knowledge, and attitude. In educating Christians to share the Gospel with Muslims, all three are needed. They need certain skills, appropriate knowledge, and the right attitude. As my ministry in Europe continues, I expect to place more emphasis on attitude then on the other two elements.

In chapter 2 it was found that a negative attitude of fear, prejudice, and suspicion towards Islam and Muslims not only characterizes Europeans in general, but is also found among Christians. If a negative attitude colors one's perception of Islam, one tends to only see the dark side of Islam and its adherents. Looking at Islam through such a negative lens, one can easily miss the transformation that takes place among Islam in Europe, as described in chapter 1.

An attitude dominated by love instead of fear tends to look for the positive instead of emphasizing the negative. Christians not only need a different set of lenses when looking at Islam or Muslims but essentially a change of heart. Such a change begins with the acknowledgement that one's negative attitude towards Muslims and Islam is a result of the sin of exclusion, as seen in chapter 2. A Christian who fears Islam and Muslims often excludes them from their heart, love, compassion, concern, interest, and life.

I concluded that a Christian's thought, attitude, and behavior with regard to Muslims should be guided by the self-giving love of God manifested at the cross of Golgotha. I also saw that what is needed for Europe to become free of *Islamophobia* are change agents, shaped by the values of God's kingdom, and capable of participating in social transformation. Christians can be such change agents when they allow the Holy Spirit to fashion in their hearts the image of the self-giving Christ.

What essentially needs to take place in the hearts of Christians is that their attitude of fear towards Islam and Muslims be replaced by an attitude of grace. Each attitude has some distinguishing characteristics:

Table 2: Characteristics of an Attitude of Fear and an Attitude of Grace

Attitude of Fear	Attitude of Grace
Suspicious of the Muslims' intentions.	Giving the Muslims the benefit of the doubt.
Exclusion of Muslims from society, the community and one's life.	Embracing the Muslims and making space for them in one's community and life.
Judgmental of the Muslims' faults and mistakes.	Willingness to acknowledge one's own shortcoming and mistakes.
Highlighting the negative in Islam.	Looking for the positive in Islam.
Uncertain about one's own identity/safety.	Identity and safety found in God.
Overlooking Muslims.	Taking Muslims seriously.
Demonizing Islam and Muslims.	Applying the Golden Rule.
Alarmism and conspiracy thinking with regard to Islam and Muslims.	Acknowledging the dark side of Islam, appreciating the good side of Islam.
Hate speech about Islam/Muslims.	Speaking well of the Muslims.
Critical of Islam.	Critical of Islam without being judgmental.
A predominantly apologetic and polemical approach to Islam and Muslims.	Willingness to enter into a dialogue with Muslims.

Attitude of Fear	Attitude of Grace
Talk about Muslims instead of with them.	Listen to Muslims with one's heart.
Generalize, stigmatize, stereotyping, dichotomize when speaking about Islam/Muslims.	Looking for the person behind the Muslim.
Closed view of Islam.	Open view of Islam.
Defend Christianity and attack Islam.	Building bridges without jeopardizing the truth and speaking the truth with love.
Considering the Muslim one's enemy.	Loving the Muslim as one loves oneself.
Unwillingness to learn from Islam/Muslims.	Willingness to learn from Islam/Muslims.
Pointing out God's judgment on Islam/Muslims.	Recognizing God's promises to Muslims and what he is doing among them.
Approach Muslims with prejudice.	Understanding the Muslim through his/her own eyes.

Although attitude change among Christians is one of the main requirements in the process of sharing the Gospel with Muslims, it was reported in chapter 3 that many of the contemporary courses and books that are written for this purpose place a higher emphasis on knowledge and skills than on attitude.[1] Several of the materials talk only or mostly about ideal or original Islam and in doing so present a predominantly closed view of present day Islam. This perception of Islam, as I concluded, is one of the characteristics of *Islamophobia*.

Several materials strongly promote an apologetic or even polemic approach towards Islam and Muslims and speak out quite negatively about an approach that includes dialogue. These factors

[1] Amy Tan and Dr. Uwe Kaufmann, "Making Good Change Agents: Attitude, Knowledge, Skills," *Six Sigma Europe*, http://www.europe.isixsigma.com/library/content/c040501a.asp/ (accessed April 14, 2009). It seems that Christians are not the only ones to overlook the attitude aspect in training change agents. It this article Tan and Kaufmann write: "When assessing potential candidates for roles as change agents, three questions need to be asked: Do they have the right attitude? Do they possess the appropriate knowledge? And do they have the necessary skills?" Commenting on the right attitude they write that attitude" is one aspect of good change agents that is often overlooked."

would make most materials less suitable to accomplish the desired change in the lives of Christians. I identified five materials that could be very helpful in bringing about this process, but found them inadequate as an introductory and easy access course for ordinary Christians.

In chapter 4 I looked at a course, which I developed, called Sharing Lives that seeks to meet all the requirements. First of all, Sharing Lives places more emphasis on attitude than on knowledge and skills. Secondly, it explicitly addresses the attitude of fear towards Islam and Muslims and helps Christians to deal with it in light of the truth of Scripture. Thirdly, it clearly promotes an attitude of grace towards Islam and Muslims. Fourthly, it includes personal interaction with Muslims, thereby avoiding talking about instead of talking with Muslims. Fifthly, it explicitly encourages participants to build relationships with Muslims. From the evaluations of the participants, which were discussed in chapter 5, I found that for over one-third of the participants this course accomplished the objective of changing their attitude towards Islam and Muslims.

The second objective of the course was that people would start building relationships with Muslims. Sixty percent of the people indicated that as a result of the course they will proactively seek to build relationships with Muslims.

In the course of conducting my research for this dissertation, I found no evidence of any analyses by other researchers with respect to how other existing courses and books have impacted the attitude of the students or readers. Consequently, it is impossible to answer the question whether the course Sharing Lives is more successful in changing people's attitude than the other materials available. I have already indicated that some of the materials available seem to increase a negative attitude towards Muslims and Islam instead of offering Christians positive solutions. Five of the materials analyzed did include many ingredients that could be used to help Christians overcome their negative attitudes. But addressing negative attitudes is not easy. People find it hard to admit their own negative attitude.[2] Sometimes they describe it in different terms.[3] I noted that it takes more than a post-training questionnaire to measure lasting transformation in people.

I do not know whether or not the participants whose attitude towards Islam and Muslims has softened will become more negative once again because of what happens in their own environment or worldwide. One can only hope that the principles of Scripture that have been communicated in the course become a permanent part of the participant's worldview.[4]

Many participants have indicated that they intend to establish contact with Muslims as a result of the course. Although I have not been able to verify whether all participants have put their intentions into action, the first feedback after four months, mentioned in the previous chapter are encouraging. There might be a need for regular follow-up and an ongoing champion to encourage people in this respect.

I have concluded that the course Sharing Lives might be a catalyst to start a process of transformation in the participant's life, while acknowledging it is by no means the only instrument that God can use to bring about attitude change in someone's life.

[2] I argued in chapter 5 that despite the condemnation of a negative attitude towards Muslims by the majority of the respondents, the main attitude that surfaces when looking at the outcome of the questionnaires is a negative one, namely: suspicion leaning towards fear.

[3] A Christian friend, whose name I can't reveal in this document, who is supportive of an extreme right political party in the Netherlands, wrote in an email to me on November 21, 2008, that he is not afraid of Islam, but simply wants to alert people to the worldwide Islamic misbehavior. He distinguishes two kinds of fears: one for spiders, which is imaginary, and one for heights. One who is afraid to jump off a roof is not afraid but sensible. This is the kind of attitude that he has towards Islam.

[4] One of the participants reflecting on the course four months later wrote that two things stand out: "1) I have begun to see Muslims as normal people and less as terrorists; 2) The emphasis in the course was on the good parts of Islam. I still find this difficult, it feels like the butter and flower of a poisonous cake are recommended. Conclusion: the Muslim human who needs Jesus and the poisonous teaching of Islam have been separated in my thoughts."

When presenting an outline of the course Sharing Lives to a group of about fifty leaders of Operation Mobilization in Europe in November 2008, I got a lot positive feedback. Several field leaders confirmed that fear of Islam is an important issue to be dealt with among Christians in Europe and have requested me to come and teach the course in several different Europeans countries. When explaining the course Sharing Lives to the director of a large denominational movement in the Netherlands in February 2009, he suggested that the material become part of their training courses. First steps have already been taken to follow up this suggestion.

Having seen that the course Sharing Lives meets a need and has helped toward a change of attitude and has encouraged people to establish relationships, it seems fair to conclude that it is a viable course, but that it is still a work in progress

Recommendations Regarding the Course Sharing Lives

In order to make the course Sharing Lives better and more effective, the following changes are recommended: (1) improve the format and content; (2) make sure there is a proper follow-up; (3) make sure the course is incorporated in the activities of churches; (4) run more pilots and do a more thorough assessment of the course; and (5) train trainers to use the course across Europe.

Improve the Format and Content

As seen in chapter 5, there are several changes that should be made to improve the course, such as: (1) more interaction in the classes; (2) more involvement of Muslims in some of the lessons, e. g. having a Muslim (co) teach lesson 3; and (3) a better integration of the content of the lectures, the notes and the homework.

Some revision needs to be done regarding the content, particularly the lesson on grace (lesson 2). The lesson as it stands at present is very much a Bible study on grace with a practical application towards Muslims. The impact of this course might improve when more of the thinking of Volf, which was discussed in chapter 2 of this dissertation, would be incorporated. In discussing the important concepts of exclusion and embrace Volf zooms in on Jesus' parable of the prodigal son. This parable should be given a more prominent place in the second lesson because it exemplifies the struggle between the costly grace and the warm embrace offered by the father and the negative attitude of exclusion shown by both sons.

Make Sure There is a Proper Follow-up

Sharing Lives is just an introductory course, focusing on the first step of a relationship between Christians and Muslims. It does not deal in depth with what comes next, that is, how to share one's faith with Muslims, how to deal with the differences between Christianity and Islam, and how to help Muslims that have come to Christ find their place in a local church. Because these are important issues that need to be dealt with, it is necessary that Sharing Lives receives the proper follow up with additional materials and courses. Some of the materials discussed in chapter 3 would be appropriate for such further training.

In order to help people follow up their desire to build relationships with Muslims as a result of taking part in the course Sharing Lives, each group needs a champion, who encourages the others to move forward. To keep this process going, it would be desirable to organize a follow up meeting every six months. During such meetings further questions and concerns that have arisen in one's relationship with Muslims could be discussed.

Make Sure the Course is Incorporated in the Activities of the Churches

As was pointed out in the introduction, one of the values behind this dissertation is that God uses his Church to carry out his plan on earth, including his plan to share his love and grace with Muslims. Consequently, it is important that whenever Sharing Lives is offered to Christians, it needs to be seen as an activity of the church, not as the hobby of individual church members. A solid incorporation of this course in a church would greatly enhance the follow-up process recommended above.

Run More Pilots and do a More Thorough Assessment of the Course

I wrote in chapter 5 that within the time constraints of this research, the main assessment of the course Sharing Lives that has taken place was level 1 of Kirkpatrick's model. In order to measure the effectiveness of this course, it is recommended that more pilots are run[5] and tools developed that enable the course to be assessed on level 2 (learning evaluation), level 3 (behavior evaluation) and level 4 (results evaluation) of Kirkpatrick's model.

Train Trainers to Use the Course Across Europe

It is recommended that, preferably after the second series of pilots and the possible additional changes made as a result of the assessments, the course be translated into other European languages and be used across Europe.[6] In order to make this intention happen a course handbook must be written and teachers must be trained.

[5] Invitations to this effect have already been received. E. g. in 2009 the course will be taught to OM colleagues in the Netherlands during several of our monthly prayer days. Also, other groups that were interested in the first pilots, are open to have the course in 2009.

[6] During the OM European Leadership Conference in November 2008, I briefly shared with my colleagues the content of the course. Afterwards several field leaders (e. g. from Poland, Austria and Denmark) contacted me and expressed interest in having the course done in their country.

Further Recommendations

In light of what has been written in this dissertation, three more recommendations are in order: (1) to monitor the development of Islam in Europe; (2) to provide a list of Best Practices of how Churches/Christians share their lives with Muslims; and (3) to identify changes in the lives of Muslims as a result of Christians sharing their lives with them.

Monitor the Development of Islam in Europe

Because the attitude of Christians towards Islam and Muslims is often influenced by the developments taking place in the world of Islam in general and Islam in Europe in particular, it is important that the changes taking place among Islam in Europe are monitored carefully by Christians. This monitoring enables us to give a balanced response against islamophobes, who only seem to be able to see the dark side of Islam.

Provide a List of Best Practices of How Churches/Christians Share their Lives with Muslims

In order to encourage Christians and churches to start sharing their lives with Muslims, it would be helpful to provide them with case studies of churches in different European cities that have successfully established bridges with Muslims. Such case studies would help Christians/churches in order to learn about a) the main ingredients of successfully establishing bridges with Muslims; b) the pitfalls to avoid when sharing your life with Muslim. Through such a list of best practices one can draw out reproducible principles to be used by Christians/churches throughout Europe.

Identify Changes in the Lives European Muslims as a Result of Contact with Christians

It is important to identify the major changes that have taken place in the lives of Muslims, their relatives, and friends as a result of their contact with Christians in Europe. It is also important to find out what key elements were responsible for these changes. Information about those elements would enable Christians to set realistic expectations for their efforts of sharing their lives with Muslims.

Every Muslim in Europe at Least One Christian Friend?

As stated in the introduction, the expected outcome of this dissertation is a process that, if implemented, could lead to my dream come true, namely to see each Muslim in Europe have at least one Christian friend.[7]

As was pointed out earlier, the number of Muslims in Europe roughly matched the number of Christians[8] in Europe, but there are several obstacles to see this dream become a reality:

1) Many Christians have negative attitude towards Islam and Muslims (and many Muslims have a negative attitude towards Christianity and Christians), with the result that the two communities often live side by side without much desire toward sharing lives. This social separation means that stereotypes about Islam and Muslims among Christians are kept alive and that structural, often religiously justified antagonism abounds.

[7] It is better to define it in this way, than to say:"Every Christian at least one Muslim friend," because it is unlikely that every Christian in Europe will be able or willing to develop a friendly relationship with a Muslim. The way it is stated namely that every Muslim has at least one Christian friend, implies that one Christian could have friendships with more than one Muslim.

[8] The term *Christian* is used in this document to define "committed, Gospel oriented, evangelical, charismatic and Pentecostal believers."

2) Many Christians have severed the Gospel from their own lives, making the Gospel a formula, a doctrine, instead of a lifestyle.
3) Many Christians have withdrawn from the world to their "Christian" island and therefore hardly participate in the society around them.
4) Many Christians have severed the social part of the Gospel from the spiritual part and therefore insufficiently pay attention to the social needs of the people around them, particularly the Muslims.
5) Friendships with Muslims can become a hindrance in sharing one's faith, because in doing do, one is afraid to lose the friendship.

Some of these obstacles have been addressed in this paper, but a lot more needs to be done. Seeing every Muslim in Europe having at least one Christian friend requires the collective effort of the whole body of Christ in Europe. This body needs to be mobilized and equipped to share their lives with the Muslims in their streets, workplaces, communities, villages and cities. Sharing the Gospel wrapped up in one's life might result in Muslims bowing their knees for the Lord of Lords and the King of Kings, Jesus, Christ and in doing so, share his eternal life. May the Holy Spirit use the course Sharing Lives as an instrument to bring about the needed change in attitude that would set this process in motion.

Appendix A
Numbers of Muslims in Europe[1]

Aus dem Europa-Archiv des Zentralinstituts Islam-Archiv-Deutschland in Soest (Stand 1. November 2006)

1. Westeuropa

Andorra	400
Belgien	400.000
Deutschland	3.293.000
Frankreich	5.500.000
Grossbritannien	1.500.000
Irland	4.000
Liechtenstein	1.527
Luxemburg	9.000
Niederlande	1.000.000
Österreich	350.000
Schweiz	330.000
Westeuropa *Gesamt*	**12.387.927**

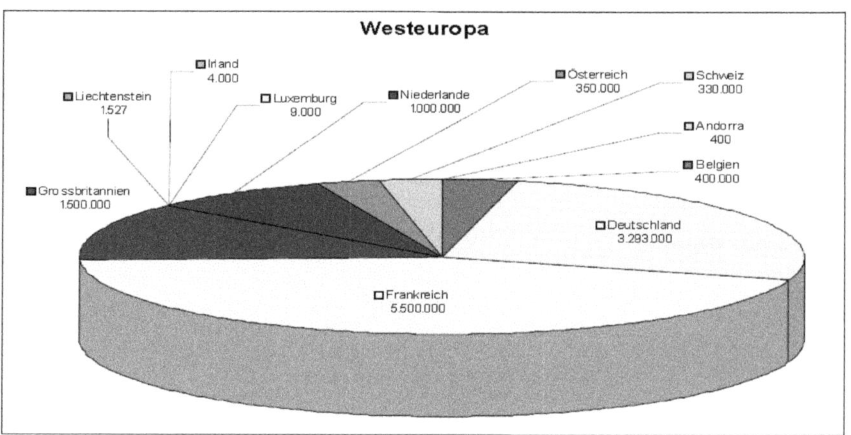

Grafik 1 Westeuropa

[1] Received in German from Mr. Gerhard Isa Moldenhauer of the Zentral Institute of Islam Archive in Germany, through e-mail on May 13, 2007.

2. Nordeuropa

Dänemark	*117.000*
Finnland	*15.000*
Island	*321*
Norwegen	*80.000*
Schweden	*250.000*
Nordeuropa Gesamt	***462.321***

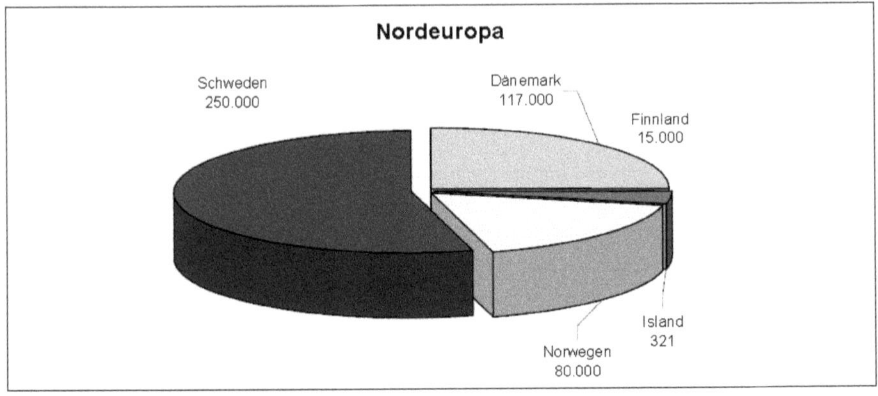

Grafik 2 Nordeuropa

3. Südeuropa

Italien	*1.000.000*
Portugal	*12.000*
Spanien	*700.000*
Malta	*4,500*
Südeuropa Gesamt	***1.716.500***

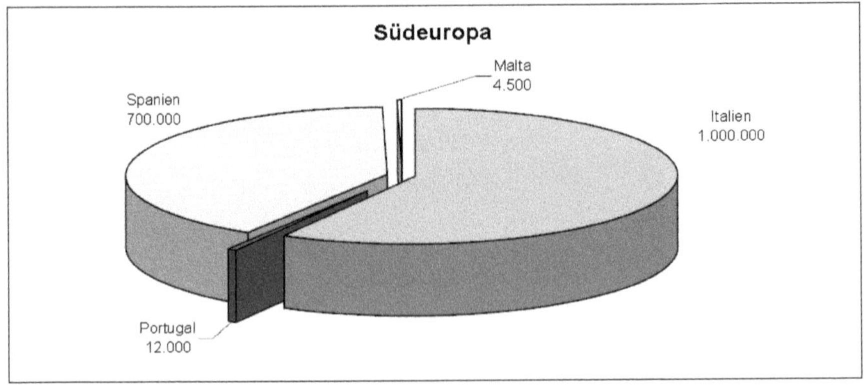

Grafik 3 Südeuropa

4. Südosteuropa

Albanien	*2.100.000*
Bosnien-Herzegowina	*2.000,000*
Bulgarien	*1,100.000*
Griechenland	*140.000*
Kroatien	*56.777*
Makedonien	*750,000*
Rumänien	*150.000*
Slowenien	*47.448*
Serbien—Montenegro (inkl. Sandschak und Kosovo)	*1.600.000*
Tschechien	*20.000*
Europ. Türkei	*5.900.000*
Ungarn	*70.000*
Zypern	*200.000*
Südosteuropa Gesamt	***14.134.225***

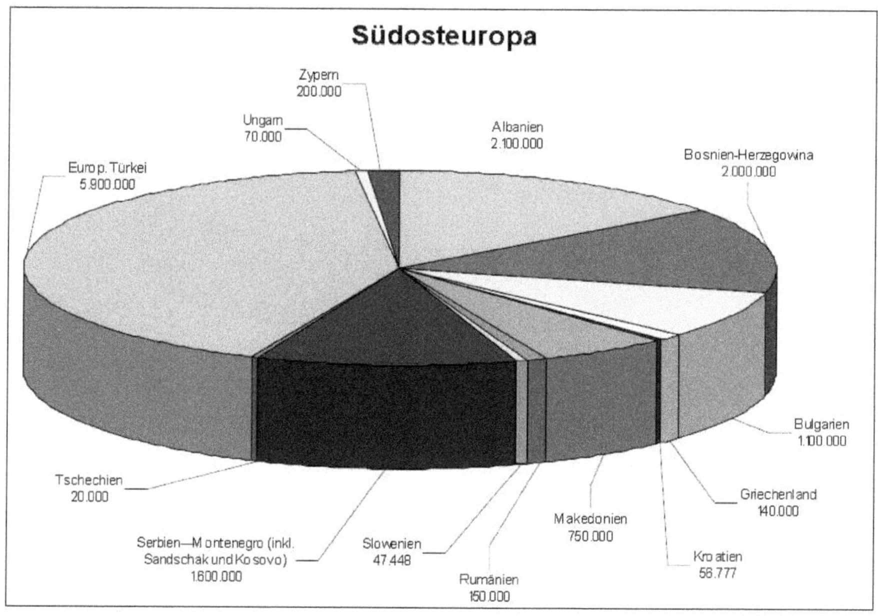

Grafik 4 Südosteuropa

5. Osteuropa

Lettland	*380*
Litauen	*5.100*
Polen	*7.500*
Russland	*25,000.000*
Osteuropa	*25,012.980*
Europa insgesamt	***53.713.953***
Davon in der Europäischen Union	***15.890.428***

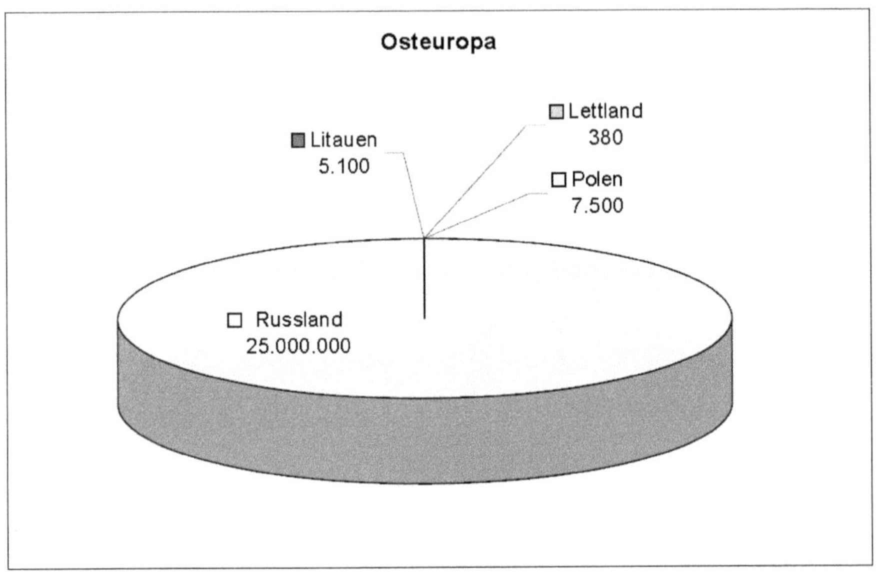

Grafik 5 Osteuropa

Anmerkung:

Die Daten widersprechen der von den deutschen Medien immer wieder aufgestellten Behauptung, es gebe keine konkreten Daten über die Zahl der Moslems in den einzelnen europäischen Ländern. Wir haben die hier aufgeführten Daten mit Hilfe der Statistischen Ämter in den einzelnen europäischen Ländern ermittelt.

Appendix B
Books and Courses Helping Christians Relate to Muslims

Book/course/	Author(s) Editor	Aims	Structure and content
Grace for Muslims, the journey from fear to faith. Milton Keynes, UK: Authentic Media, 2006, 190 pages	Steve Bell Founder of Friendship First and Director of Interserve UK.	To show that it is possible for Christians to respond to Muslims without being either theologically woolly or politically naïve. To help readers develop a nuanced understanding of Islam, discover God's heart for Muslim people and what he might be saying to the western society through the Muslim presence. To show how Christians can use the existing links between Judaism and Islam to share the good news about Jesus with Muslims.	The author's desire with the book is to enable Christians to move from prejudice to understanding, from fear to friendship, from fear of Muslims to faith for them. He does so by sharing his own struggles with the various issues presented by Islam and by writing about his own journey and reflecting upon his own process of change, when rubbing shoulders with Muslims in Egypt, United Kingdom and Africa.
Cross & Crescent: responding to the Challenge of Islam. Downers Grove, IL. USA: IVP Books, 2007, 400 pages	Colin Chapman Retired British missionary/lecturer. Worked in Egypt, Lebanon and Cyprus and UK.	To examine our own attitudes and considers the issues involved in Christian engagement with Muslims and Islam; To explore how Christians can effectively bear witness to Jesus among Muslims; To equip Christians to better understand Muslims and Islam in a rapidly changing world.	The book is divided into five parts: 1) relating to our Muslim neighbors; 2) Understanding Islam; 3 Entering into discussion and dialogue; 4) Facing Fundamental issues; 5) Bearing witness to Jesus.

Book/course/	Author(s) Editor	Aims	Structure and content
Cross and Crescent (course) London, Church Mission Society, 2003. 55 pages	Colin Chapman Developed by Colin Chapman, produced by CMS in co-operation with Faith to Faith in the UK.	To examine our own attitudes and considers the issues involved in Christian engagement with Muslims and Islam; To explore how Christians can effectively bear witness to Jesus among Muslims; To equip Christians to better understand Muslims and Islam in a rapidly changing world.	The course is build around the material of the book and designed to be covered in 5 sessions of 1½ hours each.
The Call of the Minaret Oxford University Press, 1956, 376 pages	Kenneth Cragg Author has spent some 45 years in the Middle East as professor of philosophy, as a chaplain, and as assistant bishop in the Anglican Archdiocese of Jerusalem. He has also taught at the University of Sussex, UK.	To penetrate Islam with genuine objectivity and to discover the meaning of Islam for Muslims To help Christians interpret the truth of God toward Muslims in a personal relationship	The book consists of three parts: 1) The contemporary setting, giving an overview of the developments within Islam since 1945; 2) Minaret and Muslim, looking at the concept of God, the person of Muhammad, the role of prayer and religious life in Islam and the Islamic order for human society; 3) Minaret and Christian, in which the author looks at what the Islamic call to Prayer means for the Christian, which is a call to meet, to understand, to serve, retrieve, interpret and to patience.

Book/course/	Author(s) Editor	Aims	Structure and content
The crescent through the eyes of the Cross . Colorado Springs, USA: NavPress, 2008. 261 pages.	Nabeel Jabbour Arab Christian, born in Syria, grown up in Lebanon and who lived in Egypt with his family. Works with Navigators in the US.	To help readers understand and develop compassion for Muslims. To put on Jesus and the cross as we look at and embrace the crescent in order to develop compassion and understanding.	The book is a fictional story about Ahmad, an Egyptian Muslim friend of the author. Through 'the mouth' of Ahmad and his relatives the author discusses several aspects of the Muslim worldview, such as: the relationship between Jesus Christ, Mohammad, the Qur'an and the Bible; the role of Israel, cultural differences; the role of women, the Western 'Christian' history of the Crusades en Colonialism; contextualizing our message; integrating Muslim Background Believers into the church. These issues are divided into three categories: a) the (Christian) message; b) the (Christian) messenger; c) the (Muslim) receiver.
Ask your Muslim friend Edleen, South Africa: AcadSA Publishing, 2008, 194 pages.	Andreas Maurer Swiss theologian who lives in Switzerland, where he is involved in Christian-Muslim encounters.	To give Christians an introduction to Islam and guide them for interaction with Muslims. To equip Christians to be more effective in their witness to Muslims.	The book is divided into three parts: 1) Islamic teaching; 2) Christian answers to Muslim objections: 3) Encounters with Muslims.

Book/course/	Author(s) Editor	Aims	Structure and content
Muslims and Christians at the Table New Jersey: P & R. Publishing Company, 1999, 326 pages.	Bruce McDowell and Anees Zake North American Christian leaders. Written with the North American context in mind	To promote a journey of understanding between Christians and Muslims. To set forth the historical, cultural, and theological background of Islam as a foundation for witnessing to Muslims. To encourage witnessing to North American Muslims with the gospel. To teach how to witness to them more effectively by promoting biblical understanding.	The book is divided into four parts: 1) The Vision, which answers the question why Christians in North America should reach Muslims there; 2) Understanding Muslims' Background, particularly focusing on the historical and cultural background; 3) Theological Understanding, which deals with several theological differences between Islam and Christianity; 4) Reaching Muslims, providing the theological basis and several guidelines for Muslim Evangelism.
Faith to Faith Intervarsity Press, UK, 2001, 327 pages.	Chawkat Moucary UK citizen, born in a Christian family in Syria. Consultant with World Vision.	To examine the claims of Christianity and Islam To compare several key elements of the Christian faith and the Muslim faith.	The book is divided into five parts. Part 1 looks at the Bible and the Qur'an and addresses the question whether the Biblical text has been falsified. Part 2 compares what Islam and Christianity teach about God, sin, salvation and the kingdom of God. In part 3, the different perspectives on Jesus are investigated. Part 4 looks at the prophet hood of Muhammad from a Muslim and Christian perspective. Part 5 addresses two contemporary issues that are important in Christian-Muslim relationships: Israel/ Palestine and the presence of Muslim immigrants in Europe.

Book/course/	Author(s) Editor	Aims	Structure and content
Islam: the Challenge to the Church Wiltshire, UK: Isaac Publishing, 2006. 125 pages	Patrick Sookhdeo International Director of Barnabas Fund, a charity which assists persecuted Christians particularly in the Muslim World.	To help Christians in the West to understand Islam and the challenge which the rise of Islam in the West poses to the Church.	The book gives brief basic information on Islam, Muhammad, the Qur'an and some aspects of the Islamic worldview. It discusses some of the main theological differences between Islam and Christianity. It presents several issues related to Islam and its presence in the West e. g. education, treatment of women, shari'a law, politics and media. It discusses several ways that Christians should or should not interact with Muslims.
Distinctly Welcoming Scripture Union Australia, 2007, 160 pages	Richard Sudworth Consultant with Faith to Faith in the UK. Based in a Muslim area of Birmingham.	To help the Christian communities in Britain live and work within a multi-ethnic neighborhood and to reach out to people of other faiths	The book addresses the nature of religions, the meaning of the Gospel, evangelism, community service, youth work and politics. Each chapter includes a Bible passage that is relevant for the subject of the passage, a responsive prayer, several suggested activities and questions for further reflection and references to further resources that deal with the subject of the chapter.

Book/course/	Author(s) Editor	Aims	Structure and content
Friendship First Market Rasen, UK: Friendship First Publications, 2003. 84 pages.	Steve Bell Founder of Friendship First and Director of Interserve UK.	To help ordinary Christians to relate positively to ordinary' Muslims. To get the reader to friendship with a Muslim.	The manual is divided into four sections: 1) This religion called Islam; 2) Barriers to Christian witness; 3) From friendship to fellowship; 4) Helpful appendices.
Developing a Heart for Muslims AWM and C. A. M. E. L Dos Carter, USA, Arab World Ministries and C. A. M. E. L., Institute of TechKnowledgy, 2007.	Dos Cartor (editor) Course put together by Arab World Ministries USA, in collaboration with several other organizations and developed by Rev. Dos Carter.	To help Christians: (1)identify the various branches and beliefs in Islam worldwide; (2)become familiar with Mohammad, Islam's origins, historical development, Islamic law and some of the main Islamic issues; (3)learn the basics of Islamic worship and practices focusing on gaining a clear understanding of Islamic terminology and the disparity between 'ideal' Islam and 'real' Islam.	The material is divided into five subjects: 1) Muslim Beliefs and Practices; 2) Muslim Acts of Worship; 3) Islamic Sources of Authority; 4) Mohammad's Islam; 5) Islam's Crisis of Faith. About half of the study workbooks consist of Addendums explaining issues about Islam (e. g. the meaning of Jihad, the Muslim calendar) in more detail.
Engaging with Islam Kingsford, Australia: Australian Fellowship of Evangelical Students, 2006.	Samuel Green Staff worker of the Australian fellowship of Evangelical Students.	To equip Christians 1) to understand Islam; 2) to engage effectively with Muslims; 3) to stand firm as a Christian, to defend the gospel.	The course syllabus is: ›› Dawah; Session 6: Contend for the Faith; Session 7: Evangelism

Book/course/	Author(s) Editor	Aims	Structure and content
Carey Course in Christian-Muslim Relations. London, UK: London Bible College, 2001, 320 pages.	Elsie Maxwell (editor) Published under the auspices of the Centre for Islamic Studies and Muslim-Christian Relations of London Bible College in London, UK.	To give information about Islam which will help Christians address Muslim perspectives, questions and challenges. To help Christians understand why and how they can engage in evangelism with Muslims.	There are 20 study topics in the course, divided into 2 modules: *Module I*: 1) Muhammad; 2) The Qur'an; 3) Muslim Life Style; 4)The Beliefs of Islam; 5)Pillars of Islam; 6) History; 7)Islamic Law; 8)Muslim Sects; 9)Sufism; 10)Folk Islam *Module II*: 1) Who is God? 2) Who is Jesus? 3) Salvation and Judgment; 4) Apologetics; 5) Islam outside the Arab world; 6) Festivals and Ceremonies; 7) Women in Islam; 8) Cross-cultural Communication; 9) Methodology for Ministry; 10) Care of the Worker and the Convert.
Life Challenge materials Nairobi, Kenya: Life Challenge Africa, 2006.	Gerard Nehls, Walter Eric Leaders of Life Challenge Africa, a ministry of SIM, to reach Muslims in Africa.	To equip Christians to understand the difference between Islam and the Christian faith and the way Muslims think, feel, believe and do things. To show how Muslims are taught to perceive or understand the Bible. To help Christians answer Muslim objections to the Christian faith To encourage to reach Muslims with the Gospel.	The materials consist of *Reach Out*, a 115 page, A5 size, training handbook and three Trainer's Textbooks of about 150 pages (A4-size), namely: 1. Islamics: Basis Aspects Islam; 2. Apologetics: Christian-Islamic Controversy; 3. Pragmatics: Practical-Tactical Approach.

Book/course/	Author(s) Editor	Aims	Structure and content
Encountering the World of Islam Colorado Springs, US: Authentic Publishing, 2008, 574 pages.	Keith Swartley (ed.) The course is developed under the auspices of Caleb Project, by a team of people led by editor Keith Swartley. The course textbook, includes articles of more than 80 authors	To help believers connect relationally with the Muslim community and to respectfully explain our hope in Jesus Christ, while not repeating prideful errors of the past. To provide a biblical perspective on God's heart for Muslims. To provide participants with a working knowledge of the Islamic faith. To equip participants to reach out to Muslims with the love of Christ and to explain their beliefs to Muslims.	The course is divided into four parts with three lessons each: *Part 1—The Development of Islam*: 1. The Founding of Islam; 2. The Expansion of Islam; 3. Islamic Beliefs. *Part 2—Expressions of Islam: 4. Muslims Today*; 5. The Everyday Life of Muslims; 6. The spiritual World of Muslims. *Part 3—Christianity and Islam*: 7. Cultural Barriers; 8. Theological Issues; 9. Past Approaches to Outreach. *Part 4—Our Response to Islam*: 10. Church Planting and Contextualization; 11. Our Response to Islam; 12. Prayer for the Muslim World.

Appendix C
An Outline of the Lessons of the Course Sharing Lives

Lesson 1: Understanding our fear of Islam

One of the main obstacles for sharing our lives with Muslims is fear of Islam and Muslims, together with prejudice, anxiety and suspicion. Therefore, we will look at this in some detail during this lesson.

Objectives

- To look at Jonah's unwillingness to be God's servant among his enemies in Nineveh.
- To articulate and discuss our fear (and related attitudes of anxiety, prejudice, and suspicion) and our questions and concerns of Islam or Muslims and understand the justification of these.
- To look at our fear of Islam in light of God's Word of Isaiah 40–54.

Outcome

By the end of this lesson, the student will be able to bring their fear of Islam and Muslims to the right proportion and looking at it in the shadow of the glory of our Sovereign Creator.

Outline

Introduction of the course	5 mins
Getting to know each other	10 mins
Read Jonah 1; discuss the reasons Jonah didn't want to go to Nineveh	10 mins

Answer the following questions (write the answers on a piece of paper): 10 mins
When you think of Islam, what are some of the words, images, pictures, and thoughts that come to mind?
Finish the following sentence

When it comes to Islam, I fear . . .,
I suspect that . . .

I find it unfair that . . .

Discuss answers and give examples of the justification of our fear 20 mins
DVD *Inside Islam*, part 6 10 mins
Study Isaiah 40–54: Fearing the Lord more than men or circumstances 25 mins

Home work

The main homework to be taken from this lesson and in preparation for the next is prayer in order to bring one's expressed fears into God's presence. The student is encouraged to bring his/her fears, concerns and anger about Islam to God in prayer during the next seven days using the following Psalms to guide their prayers: Day 1: Psalm 27; Day 2: Psalm 55; Day 3: Psalm 56; Day 4: Psalm 69; Day 5: Psalm 91; Day 6: Psalm 109; Day 7: Psalm 137. In some of these Psalms the psalmist brings his anger for what others have done to him before the Lord

Lesson 2: Developing a Grace Response to Muslims

Christianity's unique feature among world religions is grace. (C. S. Lewis)

When we continue to bring our fear (including our fear of Islam) into the presence of God, there comes room to develop another attitude towards Islam and Muslims, namely that of grace.

Objectives

- To pay attention to the grace of God in Jonah's life (chapter 2) and his unwillingness to be a channel of this grace (chapter 4).
- To understand the importance of grace of God in the Bible and in our own lives.

Outcome

By the end of this lesson the student will have learned what it means to develop a grace response towards Islam and Muslims.

Outline

Feedback from last lesson's home work	10 mins
Read Jonah 2:1–10 and Jonah 4:1–4 and discuss the difference between grace Jonah received (ch2) and what he was willing to give to others (ch4)	10 mins
Defining grace G (God's), R (Riches) A (At) C (Christ's) E (Expense)	15 mins

A. Grace is part of who God is
   - We find the grace of God throughout the Bible
   - Jesus is the ultimate manifestation of God's grace
   - The Spirit of God is called the Spirit of grace
   - The Gospel is called 'the Gospel of God's grace'
   - The Word of God is called 'the word of His grace'

B. Grace is related to all main doctrines in the Bible
   - We are justified by grace
   - We are saved by grace
   - We are forgiven, redeemed, adopted as God's children by grace
   - We are called by grace
   - Our future hope and eternal security based on grace

- Grace is costly
- We are what we are by grace

C. Extending grace, becoming conveyers, dispensers of grace 15 mins
- Grace empowers us to live changed, godly lives
- Grace prevents us from becoming bitter and sets us free to forgive and let go
- Grace reminds us to stay humble
- Grace gives us supernatural strength to deal with difficult circumstances
- Grace influences the way we speak
- Grace enables us to give (of) ourselves to others

DVD *Inside Islam*, part 4 10 mins

Developing a grace response towards Muslims 30 mins

- Apply the Golden Rule
- Loving our Muslim neighbor as we love ourselves
- Not to give false testimony about my (Muslim) neighbor
- A willingness to recognize the positive aspects of Islam
- Ability to view Muslims as human beings
- Seeing what God is doing among Muslims and his promises to them in the Bible

Homework

Take the prayer of St. Francis and incorporate it in your prayers in the coming week

Lord, make me an instrument of your peace,
Where there is hatred, let me sow love;
where there is injury, pardon;
where there is doubt, faith;
where there is despair, hope;
where there is darkness, light;
where there is sadness, joy;

O Divine Master, grant that I may not so much seek to be consoled as to console;

to be understood as to understand;
to be loved as to love.

For it is in giving that we receive;
it is in pardoning that we are pardoned;
and it is in dying that we are born to eternal life.

Lesson 3: Understanding Muslims

After we have faced our attitude and emotions we are in a better position to receive accurate information about Islam and Muslims.

Objectives

- To provide the student with accurate information about key aspects of Islam
- To look at what Islam teaches about the prophet Jonah

Outcome

By the end of this session the students will have accurate information about some key aspects of Islam.

Outline

Feedback from last session's home work	10 mins
DVD *Inside Islam*: part 1	15 mins
Read several sura's from the Qur'an and study what Islam teaches about Jonah	10 mins
Video clip "I am a Muslim"	5 mins

PowerPoint presentation about the following aspects of Islam:

- Origins of Islam
- Muhammad
- The expansion of Islam
- What Muslims Believe
- The Five Pillars of Islam

- Authority in Islam
- Branches and movements within Islam
- Islamic Culture and Customs
- How Muslims view Christians

Time of interaction and discussion 25 mins

Homework

Prepare for next lesson by listing some questions you would want to ask the Muslims we will be meeting about his/her faith.

Lesson 4: Meeting with Muslims

"*Courage is grace under pressure.*"—*Ernest Hemingway*

Objectives

- To have students meet and interact with Muslims, to learn about their faith, their lives.
- To encourage students to ask intelligent questions of Muslims
- To have students reflect on the responses they heard

Outcome

By the end of this session the student will have had an opportunity to meet and interact with Muslims about their faith.

Outline

Meeting with Muslims

Homework

What is it that you learned the most and appreciated the best about the faith of the Muslim you met? Read Acts 10 and reflect on the relationship between Cornelius en Peter. Compare with the

Muslims you have met. Do you think that God answers their prayers? What do you think happens when they pray? Peter learned an important lesson from Cornelius. What have you learned from the Muslims you have met? Cornelius only needed one vision to move to action, while Peter needed three. To what extent are you aware that Christians can be more resistant to what God is saying than are others outside the church?

Lesson 5: Building Relationships that Last

Objectives

- To help people understand the importance of relational and incarnational witness
- To encourage the student to proactively build meaningful relationships with Muslims that will enable them to share Jesus Christ with them.
- To provide the student with suggestions and tools that help him/her to develop a friendship with a least one Muslim.

Outcome

At the end of this session, the student should be able to start developing a friendship with at least one Muslim.

Outline

Feedback from last session's home work	10 mins
What is incarnational or relational witness?	10 mins
Do's and Don'ts in relationship with Muslims	10 mins
When sharing the Gospel	10 mins
Presenting a model of meetings and dialogue, based on Luke 2	10 mins
Practical ways to connect naturally with Muslims	10 mins
Evaluation, feedback and homework	10 mins
DVD: Dreams and Visions: story of Khalil	10 mins

Homework

Ask God to guide you to one Muslim whom he wants you to develop a relationship with for his glory.

Appendix D
Questionnaire about Islam and Muslims

	Statement	strongly agree	Agree	neutral	disagree	strongly disagree
1	Islam is tolerant to other cultures					
2	Islam is a threat to our civilization					
3	Islam is opposite to the western way of life					
4	Islam will also go through a process of secularization					
5	Muslims have the right to practice their religion in the Netherlands					
6	For Muslims jihad means to subjugate foreign lands and people					
7	Islam is the biggest threat to our national identity					
8	Islam encourages violence against non-Muslims					
9	Islam is and should be part of our multi-cultural society					
10	Most Muslim immigrants don't want to integrate in Europe					
11	I don't mind having Muslims in our local or national governments					
12	Muslims have the right to build mosques in the Netherlands					
13	I dislike the growing negative sentiments against Muslims in the Netherlands					
14	Islam is a religion of peace					
15	Muslims do not show their real face until they are a majority					
16	We need to give Muslims the benefit of the doubt					
17	Muslims are destroying our culture					
18	Islam is a religion of aggression and violence					
19	The growth of the number of Muslims is dangerous for the freedom of Christians					
20	In 30 years Europe has more liberal Muslims than conservative Muslims					
21	Muslims will destroy our democratic system, if they could.					

	Statement	strongly agree	Agree	neutral	disagree	strongly disagree
22	Religious activities of Muslims should be restricted in our country					
23	Typically Muslim are violent, aggressive and fanatical					
24	Those who have a negative attitude towards Muslims should be condemned					
25	The government should restrict the entry of Muslims in our country					
26	I don't feel bothered if Muslims are my colleagues or neighbors					
27	Typically Muslims are devout and generous					
28	The Qur'an encourages terrorism					
29	Religious Muslims can be good, loyal citizens of the Netherlands					
30	There are areas in society where Muslims and Christians can work together					
31	Most Muslims are non-violent and peaceful					
32	There is a lot that Christians can learn from Islam					
33	Muslims' civilization is as good and high as western civilization					
34	It is because of Islam that there are troubles in Israel					
35	Muslim extremists (e. g. Taliban, Al Qaeda) represent true Islam					
36	Most Muslims can't be trusted					
37	Islam's desire is to take over our country					
38	I rather see empty church buildings made into mosques than used for other purposes or being broken down					
39	Geert Wilders is right about the growing Islamization of the Netherlands and Europe					
40	The Qur'an encourages violence against Christians					
41	If nothing changes, there will be more Muslims than Christians in the Netherlands in 40 years.					
42	When I talk about Muslims with my friends, my words usually are mild					
43	Muhammad was a warlord, so fighting is part of what Islam is					
44	The media give a fair picture of Islam					

Appendix E
Outcome Pre-Course Questionnaire on Islam and Muslims

	Statement	**strongly agree**	**Agree**	**neutral**	**disagree**	**strongly disagree**
1	Islam is tolerant to other cultures	4	6	12	17	6
2	Islam is a threat to our civilization	5	16	15	8	1
3	Islam is opposite to the western way of life	8	24	11	2	
4	Islam will also go through a process of secularization	3	13	13	10	1
5	Muslims have the right to practice their religion in the Netherlands	7	31	5	4	
6	For Muslims jihad means to subjugate foreign lands and people	7	8	12	13	2
7	Islam is the biggest threat to our national identity	5	7	17	10	5
8	Islam encourages violence against non-Muslims	4	20	10	11	2
9	Islam is and should be part of our multi-cultural society	1	20	5	17	4
10	Most Muslim immigrants don't want to integrate in Europe	3	17	9	15	2
11	I don't mind having Muslims in our local or national governments	3	22	10	9	2
12	Muslims have the right to build mosques in the Netherlands	2	25	8	5	3
13	I dislike the growing negative sentiments against Muslims in the Netherlands	4	16	15	6	3
14	Islam is a religion of peace	1	6	11	21	7
15	Muslims do not show their real face until they are a majority	4	13	15	12	1
16	We need to give Muslims the benefit of the doubt	1	12	17	9	6
17	Muslims are destroying our culture	3	6	16	20	2
18	Islam is a religion of aggression and violence	3	6	18	10	3
19	The growth of the number of Muslims is dangerous for the freedom of Christians	3	23	10	9	1
20	In 30 years Europe has more liberal Muslims than conservative Muslims	1	15	19	10	
21	Muslims will destroy our democratic system, if they could.	4	13	10	15	1

	Statement	strongly agree	Agree	neutral	disagree	strongly disagree
22	Religious activities of Muslims should be restricted in our country	5	9	14	16	2
23	Typically Muslim are violent, aggressive and fanatical	4	8	5	23	6
24	Those who have a negative attitude towards Muslims should be condemned	11	18	6	7	5
25	The government should restrict the entry of Muslims in our country	2	10	12	18	4
26	I don't feel bothered if Muslims are my colleagues or neighbors	5	26	7	8	1
27	Typically Muslims are devout and generous	2	19	18	7	1
28	The Qur'an encourages terrorism	4	11	19	11	2
29	Religious Muslims can be good, loyal citizens of the Netherlands	5	31	7	1	1
30	There are areas in society where Muslims and Christians can work together	5	33	3		2
31	Most Muslims are non-violent and peaceful	4	25	7	8	2
32	There is a lot that Christians can learn from Islam	5	10	12	15	4
33	Muslims' civilization is as good and high as western civilization		12	14	14	4
34	It is because of Islam that there are troubles in Israel	7	8	18	12	1
35	Muslim extremists (e. g. Taliban, Al Qaeda) represent true Islam	2	6	8	21	14
36	Most Muslims can't be trusted	4	8	7	17	6
37	Islam's desire is to take over our country	2	11	14	13	5
38	I rather see empty church buildings made into mosques than used for other purposes or being broken down	2	2	13	21	8
39	Geert Wilders is right about the growing Islamization of the Netherlands and Europe	4	24	13	4	2
40	The Qur'an encourages violence against Christians	4	18	15	8	2
41	If nothing changes, there will be more Muslims than Christians in the Netherlands in 40 years.	3	28	11	4	
42	When I talk about Muslims with my friends, my words usually are mild	3	20	16	8	
43	Muhammad was a warlord, so fighting is part of what Islam is	2	18	21	12	2
44	The media give a fair picture of Islam	2	6	12	14	2

Appendix F
Evaluations Course Sharing Lives

Underneath is an overview and analysis of the responses to the evaluation questionnaire that was handed out to the participants of the course *Sharing Lives* during the last session of the course.

Question 1: What have you gained the most from this course?

The answers can be divided into four categories: 1) the importance of relationship in witnessing about our Christian faith with Muslims; 2) to have an open view of Islam; 3) to change our attitude towards Islam/Muslims; and 4) skills for evangelizing Muslims. Underneath are all the answers given to this question.

Importance of relationship in witnessing about our Christian faith with Muslims (9)	**To have an open view of Islam (11)**	**To change our attitude towards Islam/Muslims (9)**	**Skills for evangelizing Muslims (4)**
That you have to get in touch with people in order to reach them with the Gospel.	Islam is not a solid block, the same for everyone, but a Muslim is a human being of flesh and blood, for whom Islam has a personal meaning	I was made aware of unspoken prejudices	learn what to do and not to do
Practical suggestions on how to get in touch with Muslims.	learn to take their culture into consideration	A far less we–they attitude	Practical tools to speak with Muslims.
Practical suggestions on how to relate to Muslim	I didn't know there were so many linkages between Islam and Christianity. This could be a good start to speak about our message.	Awareness of my attitude towards Muslims/Islam;	That you can be very open about your faith when dealing with Muslims.

Importance of relationship in witnessing about our Christian faith with Muslims (9)	**To have an open view of Islam (11)**	**To change our attitude towards Islam/Muslims (9)**	**Skills for evangelizing Muslims (4)**
Go to them and make contact.	That Islam acknowledges the Bible (OT) as a holy book	What should be our attitude?	I have learned how to evangelize a Muslim.
How to relate to Muslims and how to share our faith with them.	That it is important to approach Muslims in a positive way, because it is possible to have conversations about our faith	The importance of one's own attitude towards Muslims.	
How we as Christians can relate with Muslims.	I have gained much understanding of Muslims' idea of doing what they have been doing against other religions, especially Christians.	The knowledge I have acquired also has put no fear in me for approaching them.	
A discussion is not helpful (which confirms what I knew).	I have learned that Islam is not that barbaric religion as portrayed in the media or other avenues but rather a peaceful religion whose image has been tarnished by a few fanatics.	It has softened my heart for Muslims. This is, it has opened my eyes to the fact that God loves them too and He wants them to be saved.	
To have good relationship with Muslims.	This course has really helped me to understand Muslim life.	Through the grace of God, God can save the Muslims as well.	
This course has helped me to get access to build relationship with Muslim friends.	My ability to see Muslims as I see myself irrespective of the fact that we have different beliefs	My view of evangelizing to the Muslims has changed.	

Importance of relationship in witnessing about our Christian faith with Muslims (9)	To have an open view of Islam (11)	To change our attitude towards Islam/Muslims (9)	Skills for evangelizing Muslims (4)
	My perception of Muslims has been changed.		
	Knowledge of Islam/ Muslims.		

Question 2: Mention at least one thing you will do as a result of attending this course

The answers to this question can be divided into four categories: 1) to establish contact with Muslims; 2) to speak differently about and relate differently with Muslims; 3) to study more about Islam; and 4) other. Underneath are all the answers given to this question.

To establish contact with Muslims (16)	To speak differently about and relate differently with Muslims (3)	To study more about Islam (4)	Other (1)
Get in touch with Muslims in my town. I already wanted to do this, but now I have a better understanding of how.	To not emphasize too much the negative aspects of Islam	To study the worldview of the Muslims even more.	I will devote my time to prayer at least three times a day.
More contact with my Muslim neighbor (sit, ask, listen); probably a language course with Muslims (Turkish/Moroccan women); in my own life more practically sharing my Christian faith.	I will listen and be patient with my interaction with Muslims.	To read the book Cross and Crescent very good; not much further.	
To make more contact with Muslims.	I will embrace any Muslim who comes my way	I also would like to read the Quran.	

To establish contact with Muslims (16)	To speak differently about and relate differently with Muslims (3)	To study more about Islam (4)	Other (1)
I know better how to relate to Muslims; during my internship (with predominantly Moroccan boys) I hope to be able to use this knowledge.		I will start from now at least attending some seminars on such issues.	
In February I hope to do my internship in an Islamic country; I can use this course to help me building relationships with Muslims.			
To establish contact with Muslims and learn about their customs without a preconceived meaning.			
To approach Muslims more openly and to put aside my prejudices and develop a relationship.			
To start the conversation about our faith and be hospitable for my house mate whom I see in the weekends. She is a Muslim from Azerbaijan.			

To establish contact with Muslims (16)	To speak differently about and relate differently with Muslims (3)	To study more about Islam (4)	Other (1)
I will cultivate a friendly and cordial relationship with Muslims and my evangelism to them will be by my lifestyle portraying Jesus and the gospel in an attractive way.			
I will pray to God to send a Muslim on my way just like you met the guy in the bus/ train so that I can start building relationship with him.			
I will invite some Muslim friends into my house.			
Evangelism for a better interaction between Christians and Muslims.			
Pray to God to grant me the opportunity to convert Muslim friends to Christianity.			
To make sure that I will be closer to at least one Muslim			
To start looking for a way to build a relationship with a Muslim.			
To share the love of Christ with Muslims I meet on the street.			

Question 3: In which of the three following areas has the course been most helpful to you: Knowledge on Islam/Muslims; Attitude towards Islam/Muslims; Skills to relate with Muslims

Attitude: 8
Skills: 7
Knowledge: 3
Knowledge and Skills: 3
Attitude and Skills: 2
All three: 1

Question 4: Think of five very different people you will meet after this course. What will you tell them about it?

The answers to this question can be divided into four groups: 1) some would say they obtained knowledge; 2) others mentioned they would say they have learned about attitude; 3) others would say they have acquired certain skills; 4) other participants had other answers. Underneath are all the answers given to this question.

I have obtained knowledge (7)	**I have learned about attitude (14)**	**I have acquired skills (7)**	**Other (3)**
It is good to learn more about this. It is solid material and important to learn more about Muslims.	The course makes you aware of your attitude towards Muslim.	Provides practical suggestions on how to contact Muslims.	This course is worthwhile.
A small-scale course that helps you to understand the background of Islam and provides you with tools to evangelize them. A personal course that makes you think.	That we should not be afraid of Islam and that there are many possible bridges between Christians and Muslims.	When you want to learn how to relate in a good way with Muslims this course is worthwhile.	When you already know a lot about Muslims and the Qur'an, it is an interesting course.

I have obtained knowledge (7)	I have learned about attitude (14)	I have acquired skills (7)	Other (3)
That many prophets of the Bible are also acknowledged in Islam.	Makes me think about my prejudices etc.	We should not be afraid of Islam and that there are many possible bridges between Christians and Muslims.	I have started greetings my Muslims friends in Arabic. I have also been discussing this course with my pastor. I have also told some of my Muslim colleagues about this wonderful course.
That it is a good course where you learn about Islam and Muslims and about biblical perspectives of relating to people of other faiths.	It made me more aware of my attitude; how much am I really open for a conversation with Muslims; what do I show myself?	Good course that teaches you to relate to Muslims.	
Particularly the last two lessons I learned a lot (*the last two lessons were about Islam and how to develop relationships with Muslims BdR)*	If the person I will talk to is happening to be a Christian, I will tell him, it is the way we Christians have negative thoughts about Muslims; the same way they also have a much more negative things against our Christian religion	Interesting. Learned a lot about possibilities to develop relationships and evangelism.	
My knowledge on Islam and attitude towards Muslims.	God loves the Muslims and wants them saved. We need not judge Muslims but treat them with compassion and respect.	The course gives tools about speaking with Muslims.	
To learn to know more about Islam and how we can share the Gospel to the Muslims.	We should try to understand Muslims and why they believe what they believe.	To learn to know more about Islam and how we can share the Gospel to the Muslims.	

I have obtained knowledge (7)	I have learned about attitude (14)	I have acquired skills (7)	Other (3)
	This is a very good course and has helped me to change my attitude towards Muslims as bad people. Therefore they should try to take part.		
	Tell them of my experience at the mosque as a practical thing to tolerant they were in answering questions when Christians interact with them.		
	My knowledge on Islam and attitude towards Muslims.		
	Never to hate Muslims as a result of some few others who misconduct themselves.		
	The special grace of God is available to all.		
	The way we portray the image of the Muslims is not the way they are.		
	That the course is an eye-opener. That Muslims and Christians have one origin from the Bible. It was a very educative course.		

Question 5: What do you think will you remember most about this course? Why?

Most people mentioned that the visit to the mosque was the more memorable of the course, others referred to aspects of the content of the course, and particularly about one's attitude towards Islam/Muslims and relating with them while others mentioned other highlights. Underneath are all answers to this question.

The visit to the mosque (12)	**The content of the course (10)**	**Other (3)**
Visit to the mosque; imam looked sincere; it's is about people; people whom Jesus loves.	Practical suggestions on how to contact Muslims.	The PowerPoint presentations are very good.
Visit to the mosque; good and educative.	I think that attitude and forms of relating will stay.	The enthusiasm of Bert and how he shares his faith; this puts me to think and makes me enthusiastic. He speaks from experience which makes things come alive.
The visit to the mosque; it was the first time for me and I liked it; I liked the conversation there.	The story of Jonah. How he was sent to Nineveh by God to preach the word.	The way you explain the outlines are perfect and I have learnt something good also.
The visit to the mosque, because this was new; and that I can put what I've learned into practice.	That God wants us to reach the Muslims and unlike Jonah in the Bible who was judgmental we need to view Muslims in a more positive way just like God sees them.	
To enter into a dialogue with Muslims, because relationships are very important when reaching Muslims with the Gospel	That I will share my life experiences with Muslims to attract them.	

The visit to the mosque (12)	The content of the course (10)	Other (3)
The visit to the mosque because it made it clear that Muslims in several ways think similar to us. Also the faith of this people is strongly imbedded in their lives and I can learn from this.	How to deal with the Muslims; why: before it is through this course I got to know more about Muslims and Islam together with going to the mosque.	
The visit to the mosque. I found it interesting that these young people deal with their faith in similar ways than we do. At the same time to realize that theirs is totally wrong (at least in my eyes).	That we need to have time to evangelize the Muslims.	
The visit to the mosque; I had never been to a mosque and spoken with an imam.	Very educative. Never to have a prejudiced mind about something without finding the true cause.	
Our interview with the Muslim leaders at the mosque. I understand most of the violence we think it is being caused by Muslims; it isn't so. Most of these violence and killing is being done by the politicians in the name of Islam.	How should we behave and relate to Muslims and through that they might come to the faith in Jesus Christ.	
I will remember the visit to the mosque. It was my first time of entering a mosque.	Ishmael sacrificed to God instead of Ishak.	
The visiting of the mosque because I had a privilege to ask questions which I had no explanation before then.		
How to deal with the Muslims; why: before it is through this course I got to know more about Muslims and Islam together with going to the mosque.		

Question 6: Can you suggest three ideas (however big or small) that may help to make this a better and more valuable course?

The answers given to this question can be divided into the following groups: 1) some people wanted more information on Islam; 2) some wanted more interaction in class; 3) others wanted more practical tools; 4) some wanted more interaction with Muslims and to read more from the Qur'an; 5) some had other general comments. Other participants answered this question by suggesting that the course will be promoted in more places and expanded to other churches. Underneath are the responses in the first five categories.

More information on Islam (7)	**More interaction in class (6)**	**More practical tools (4)**	**More interaction with Muslims (7)**	**General (7)**
More information about the teachings of Islam that is very contradictory to the Gospel.	First evening: very good, lot of interaction; 2nd evening lot of listening. Try to keep the interaction so that it is easier to swallow the material; a good course!	Even more focus on practical relationship with Muslims.	More meetings with Muslims (from someone who was not present during the mosque visit).	I found the questionnaire at the beginning very negative; as if people were supposed to have a negative view. This was a pity and puts people in a corner.
I would have liked to learn more of the content of Islam; in this respect I learned not much new; the things of the course I already knew.	In the lessons we've listened a lot; I would have like more interaction; this makes people more active and involved. I might have been good when there would have been more room for our questions;	Something more about Turkish and Moroccan culture.	Invite Muslims to discuss about several subjects.	Make sure you have a complete reader at the beginning; this was not easy to work with for me.

More information on Islam (7)	More interaction in class (6)	More practical tools (4)	More interaction with Muslims (7)	General (7)
	we do have some experiences and more could have been done with this.			
I would have liked to learn more about the content of Islam and how to have an in-depth conversation with them.	In the first lesson it might have been good to have people share about their own experiences and find out what we already know, before giving us a lot of information.	Give more practical tools.	The ability to use a Muslim in certain presentations.	Keep the material in one language, either Dutch or English.
More content on the worldview of Muslims and the Qur'an; more on the similarities between Muslims and Christians to use in practice.	You answer a question but do not ask whether the answer was sufficient but continue with the course, this can be difficult for introvert people.	More practice in how to answer Muslim objections (e. g. through role plays).	The visit to the mosque can be increased to more than one occasion.	Text of the material in Dutch.
More information about the beginning of Islam.	Sometimes more interaction, e. g. the last 15 minutes of each lesson.		If possible let us read from the Qur'an ourselves. I have never read the Quran in English.	The period of the lectures should be friendlier (comfortable time).
The first lessons were more about prejudices and fear and about Jonah. This was partially known to me and therefore less interesting,	Keep asking questions to the class to keep them alert.		Building a better relationship; having a chance to convert Muslims; knowing and learning about their attitude.	The ability to broaden the course in comparison with other religions like Hinduism.

More information on Islam (7)	More interaction in class (6)	More practical tools (4)	More interaction with Muslims (7)	General (7)
because I wanted to learn more about what Muslims think and how I can respond to this; therefore I particularly liked the last lessons.	Keep asking questions to the class to keep them alert.		Building a better relationship; having a chance to convert Muslims; knowing and learning about their attitude.	The ability to broaden the course in comparison with other religions like Hinduism.
I missed more information about Islam. I had had that before, so for me personally it was not a problem.			Get a convert of Muslim to Christianity and also testimonies of people who have benefited as a result of the program.	The ability to give more homework.

Bibliography

Al-Maktabi. "Islamophobia." *Salaam*. http://www.salaam.co.uk/maktabi/islamophobia.html. (accessed April 14, 2009).

Ancram, Michael. "Clash or Dialogue of Civilisations?" Speech delivered to Oxford Centre for Islamic Studies, May 16, 2003. Oxford.

Barrett, D., ed. *World Christian Encyclopedia*. Oxford: Oxford University Press, 2001.

Bell, Steve. *Friendship First: the Manual*. Market Rasen, UK: Friendship First Publications, 2003.

—. *Grace for Muslims, the journey from fear to faith*. Milton Keynes, UK: Authentic Media, 2006.

—. *Grace for Muslims? The journey from fear to faith*. Milton Keynes: Authentic Media, 2006.

Best, Ernest. *Black's New Testament Commentaries. A commentary of the First and Second Epistles to the Thessalonians*. Peabody, MA: Hendrickson Publishers, 1993.

Bowen, John R. *Why the French don't like the Headscarves: Islam, the State and Public Space*. Princeton, NJ: Princeton University Press, 2006.

Bruce, F. F. *1 and 2 Thessalonians*. Edited by Bruce M. Metzger. *Word Biblical Commentary*. Dallas: Word Incorporated, 1982.

Bunzl, Matti. "Between anti-Semitism and Islamophobia: Some thoughts on the new Europe." *American Ethnologist* 32, no. 4 (2005): 499–508.

Carey, George. "The Cross and the Crescent (the Clash of Faiths in an Age of Secularism)." September 18, 2006. The Beach Lecture, Newbold College, Bracknell.

Carr, Matt. "You are Now Entering Eurabia." *Race & class* 48, no. 1 (2006): 1–22.

Castle, Stephen. "Islamophobia Takes A Grip Across Europe." *The Independent*. http://www.independent.co.uk/news/europ/islamophobia-takes-a-grip-across-europe-429021.html. (accessed April 14,2009).

Cesari, Jocelyne. *When Islam and Democracy Meet: Muslims in Europe and the United States*. New York: Palgrave, 2004.

Chapman, Colin. "Christian Responses to Islam, Islamism and 'Islamic Terrorism'." *Cambridge Papers* 16, no.2 (June 2007):.

—. *Cross & Crescent: responding to the Challenge of Islam*. Downers Grove, IL, USA: IVP Books, 2007.

Dammen McAuliffe, Jane, ed. *Encyclopaedia of the Qur'an*. Boston: Brill, 2006.

Dos, Cartor, ed. *Developing a Heart for Muslims: an introduction to Islam*. Atlanta: C. A. M. E. L, 2007.

European Coalition for Israel. "4th Annual Policy Conference: Promoting The Reform Process In The Middle East -what Role Can The European Union Play?" *European Coalition For Israel*, September, 2006. http://www.ec4i.org/content/blogsection/6/49// (accessed April 1, 2009).

European Council for Fatwa and Research. *First collection of Fatwas*. Cairo: Islamic INC, 1999.

Fetzer, Joel and Chris Soper. *Muslims and the State in Britain, France and Germany*. Cambridge: Cambridge University Press, 2005.

Friderich, Scott. "The European Spiritual Estimate." *Emrg Home Page*, 2005. http://www.emrg.dzubinski.com/ (accessed April 14, 2009). BIBLIOGRAPHY

Glazov, Jamie. "Symposium:the Muslim Persecution Of Christians." *Frontpagemagazine*. http://www.frontpagemag.com/Articles/Read.aspx?GUID=8C1D2863-9FE5-43E9-BA8E-B21C2FFE5158/ (accessed April 14, 2009).

Gragg, Kenneth. *The Call of the Minaret*. Oxford: Oxford University Press, 1956.

Green, Samuel. *Engaging With Islam: A Training Course for Christians*. Kingsford, Australia: Australian Fellowship of Evangelical Students, 2006.

Halliday, Fred. "Islamophobia Reconsidered." *Ethnic and Racial Studies* 22, no. 5 (September 1999): 892–902.

Hartwig, Mark. "Spread By The Sword." *Answering Islam.org*. http://www.answering-islam.org/Terrorism/by_the_sword.html. (accessed April 14, 2009).

Howarth, Toby. "The Church Facing Islam in Western Europe." *Transformation* 20, no. 4 (October 2004): 229–231.

Huntington, Samuel P. *The Clash of Civilizations and the Remaking of World Order*. London: Simon & Schuster, 1997.

Hussein, Shakira. "They Do Not Vilify Our Ideas, They Vilify Us: A Reply To Salman Rushdie." *Opendemocracy.net*, February 22, 2005. http://www.opendemocracy.net/faith-multiculturalism/article_2349.jsp#/ (accessed June 8, 2008).

Inside Islam. DVD. Directed by Mark Hufnail. 100. A&E Home Video, 2003.

Jabbour, Nabeel T. *The Crescent Through the Eyes of the Cross*. Colorado Springs, CO: NavPress, 2008.

Jenkins, Philip. *God's Continent: Christianity, Islam and Europe's Religious Crisis*. Oxford: Oxford University Press, 2007.

Johnstone Patrick, Robyn Johnstone and Jason Mandryk. *Operation World*. Carlisle: Paternoster Lifestyle, 2001.

Johnstone, Penelope and Jan Slomp. "Islam and the churches in Europe: A Christian perspective." *Journal of Muslim Minority Affairs*, 18, no. 2 (October 1998): 355–364.

Keaton, Trica Danielle. *Muslim Girls and the Other France: Race, Identity Politics & Social Exclusion*. Bloomington: Indiana University Press, 2006.

Klausen, Jytte. *The Islamic Challenge: politics and religion in Western Europe*. Oxford: Oxford University Press, 2005.

Laurence Jonathan and Justin Vaisse. *Integrating Islam: Religious and Political Challenges in Contemporary France*. Washington, DC: Brookings Institute, 2006.

Leiken, Robert. "Europe's Angry Muslims." *Foreign Affairs* 84, no. 4 (July/August 2005):.

Liechty, Joseph and Cecelia Clegg. *Moving Beyond Sectarianism: Religion, Conflict and Reconciliation in Northern Ireland*. Dublin: The Colomba Press, 2001.

Lindon, Sarah. "Words On Images: The Cartoon Controversy." *Opendemocracy.net*, February 10, 2006. http://www.opendemocracy.net/content/articles/PDF/3257.pdf. (accessed June 8, 2008).

Malik, Kenan. "Islamophobia Myth." *Prospect*. http://www.prospect-magazine.co.uk/article_details.php?id=6679/ (accessed April 14, 2009).

Mamdani, Mahmood. *Good Muslim, Bad Muslim*. New York: Pantheon Books, 2004.

Maurer, Andreas. *Ask your Muslim Friend*. Edleen, South Africa: AcadSA Publishing, 2008.

Maxwell, Dr. Elsie, ed. *Carey Course in Christian-Muslim Relations*. London: London Bible College, 2001.

McDowell, Bruce and Anees Zaka. *Muslims and Christians at the Table*. New Jersey: P & R Publishing Company, 1999.

Mcgee, J. Vernon. *1 & 2 Thessalonians (Through the Bible Commentary series)*. Nashville, Tenessee: Thomas Nelson, Inc, 1995, 35ff. quoted in *http://www.preceptaustin.org/1thessalonians_21-htm*.

Modood, Tariq. "Muslims and the Politics of Difference." *Political Quarterly* 74, no. 1 (2003):.

More than Dreams. by 187. Vision Video, 2007.

Moucarry Chawkat. *Faith to Faith: Christianity & Islam in dialogue*. Nottingham: Intervarsity Press, 2001.

Musk, Bill. *Holy War, Why do some Muslims become fundamentalists?*. London: Monarch Books, 2003.

—. *Kissing Cousin? Christians and Muslims face to face*. Oxford: Monarch Books, 2005.

Nehls, Gerard and Walter Eric. *Reach Out and Trainers's Textbook*. Nairobi, Kenya: Life Challenge Africa, 2006.

Nexhat, Ibrahimi. "Islam's First Contacts With The Balkan Nations.". www.geocities.com/Athens/Delphi/6875/nexhat.html. (accessed June 1, 2007).

Nickel, Gordon D. *Peaceable Witness among Muslims*. Ontario, Canada: Herald Press, 1999.

Norris, Pipa and Roger Inglehart. "Religion and Politics in the Islamic World." In *Sacred and Secular: Religion and Politics Worldwide*. Cambridge: Cambridge University Press, 2004.

Organization of the Islamic Conference. "First Annual Report On Islamophobia." *Permanent Mission Of The Organization Of The Islamic Conference*, 2007. http://www.oic-un.org/reports.asp/ (accessed April 14, 2009).

Pauly, Robert J. *Islam in Europe: Integration or Marginalization*. Aldershot, UK: Ashgate, 2004.

Pawson, David. *The Challenge of Islam to Christians*. London: Hodder & Stoughton, 2003.

Poole,Patrick. "Islam's Global War Against Christianity." *American Thinker*. http://www.americanthinker.com/2007/07/ islams_global_war_against_chri.htmt. (accessed April 14, 2009).

Ramadan, Tariq. *To be a European Muslim*. Leicester: The Islamic Foundation, 1999.

—. *Western Muslims and the future of Islam*. Oxford: Oxford Univesity Press, 2004.

Ramberg, Ingrid. "Islamophobia And Its Consequences On Young People." *Eycb*, June, 2004. http://eych.coe.int/eycbwwwroot/HRE/eng/documents/ Islamophobia%20report/Islamophobia%final%ENG.pdf. (accessed April 14, 2009).

Riddell, Peter G. & Peter Cotterell. *Islam in Context: past, present and future*. Grand Rapids, MI: Baker Academic, 2004 (second edition).

Robinson, Ruth. "Ebr 2007 (revised).", 2007. www.emrgnet.eu/wordpress/data/ europe-level/ebr-2007/ (accessed December 28, 2008).

Rohe, Matthias. *Muslim Minorities and the Law in Europe—Changes and Challenges*. New Delhi: GM Publications, 2007.

The Runnymede Trust. *Islamophobia: a challenge for us all*. London: The Runnymede Trust, 1997.

Rushdie, Salman. "Defend The Right To Be Offended." *Opendemocracy.net*, February 7, 2005. http:www.opendemocracy.net/faith-europe_islam/ar ticle_2331.jsp#>/ (accessed June 5, 2008).

Sadikoglu, Necmi. "." Speech delivered to International Conference on Islamophobia, December 8, 2007. Istanbul.

Savage, Timothy M. "Europe and Islam: Crescent Waxing, Cultures Clashing." *The Washington Quarterly* (summer 2004): 25–50.

Showell-Rogers, Gordon. "Christians have nothing to fear of Islam." Speech delivered to General Assembly European Evangelical Alliance, October 17, 2007. Greece.

Sookhdeo, Patrick. *Islam: the Challenge to the Church*. Wiltshire, UK: Isaac Publishing, 2006.

Sudworth, Richard. *Distinctly Welcoming*. NSW, Australia: Scripture Union Australia, 2007.

Swartley, Keith E., ed. *Encountering the World of Islam*. Colorado Springs CO: Authentic Publishing, 2008.

Tan, Amy and Dr. Uwe Kaufmann. "Making Good Change Agents: Attitude, Knowledge, Skills." *Six Sigma Europe*. http://www.europe.isixsigma.com/library/content/c040501a.asp/ (accessed April 14, 2009).

Tibi, Bassam. "Europeanisation, Not Islamisation.", March 22, 2007. www.signandsight.com/features/1258.html. (accessed December 28, 2008).

Trifkovic, Serge. *The Sword of the Prophet: Islam, history, theology, impact on the world*. Boston,.: Regina Orthodox Press Inc, 2002.

Volf, Miroslav. *Exclusion and Embrace*. Nashville, TN: Abingdon Press, 1996.

Wadud, Amina. *Inside the Gender Jihad: Women's Reform in Islam*. Oxford: One World Publications, 2006.

Weller, Dr. Paul. "Addressing Religious Discrimination and Islamophobia: Muslims and Liberal Democracies, the case of the United Kingdom." *Journal of Islamic Studies* 17, no. 3 (2006): 295–325.

Woodberry, J. Dudley, G. Shubin, and G. Marks. "Why Muslims Follow Jesus." *Christianity Today*, October 24, 2007, 80–85.

Ye'or, Bat. *Eurabia: the Euro-Arab axis*. Madison, NJ: Fairleigh Dickinson University Press, 2005.

Zader, Ziauddin. "Why do they hate us?" Review of *Occidentalism: a history of anti-westernism*, by Buruma, James. *New Statesman* Muslim is not a dirty word (October 4 2004).

Zebiri, Kate. *Muslims and Christians Face to Face*. Oxford: One World Publications, 1997.

Mission and Apologetics

Peter Beyerhaus

This book is based on a series of lectures which the author delivered during the fall of 2003 as a guest professor at the prestigious Yonsei University in Seoul, Korea. Aware that the Korean Church has now taken over the lion's share of the recruitment and world-wide deployment of trans-cultural missionaries, the author seeks to equip students spiritually for the encounter with adherents of non-Christian belief systems and of anti-Christian movements. Avoiding mere alarmism, the intention is to give positive guidelines for persuasively presenting the biblical truth. Today the Gospel's claim that Jesus Christ is the way, the truth and the life, apart from whom salvation cannot be attained, is contested not only externally by rival religions and quasi-religious ideologies; it is challenged within Christendom itself by those who deny the objectivity of biblical revelation and advocate an inter-faith dialogue aiming at a mere friendly sharing of spiritual experiences.

Giving in to such a mentality severs the very roots of the Christian missionary vocation, as we see, alas, within a large segment of Western Christians today. Since the days of the Apostles and Church Fathers, evangelistic witness to and apologetic defence of the truth have always constituted two inseparable prongs of missionary outreach. The publication of these lectures is guided by the hope that the book may open many minds to the urgent relevance of this insight.

Pb. • 285 S. • 25.80 € (D) • 19.95 £ • 29.99 $ • ISBN 978-3-937965-44-4

Christian Mission in Eschatological Perspective

Lesslie Newbigin's Contribution

Jürgen Schuster

This book examines the implications of Newbigin's understanding of the Kingdom of God for his theology of mission. Newbigin's theological thinking is based on an eschatologically oriented historical understanding of revelation. The gospel tells God's story with his world. In Christ the reign of God has been revealed on earth, yet its final consummation is still to come.

Five areas are explored which are affected by this eschatological framework: (1) It provides the reference point for an integrative understanding of mission as witness in both word and deed. (2) The historical character of the revelation makes the gospel part of public truth in contrast to private truth. The gospel is neither a religious way for private salvation nor the establishment of a world immanent theocracy. (3) The church does not constitute the kingdom but is called to be "firstfruits, instrument, and sign" of God's reign. (4) The verification of the truth the church witnesses to occurs only at the end of time. (5) In the meantime the credibility of the biblical tradition can only be advocated provisionally and witnessed to in the religiously pluralistic context the church finds itself in.

Pb. • 285 S. • 24.80 € (D) • 23.80 £ • 38.70 $ • ISBN 978-3-941750-15-9

www.ingramcontent.com/pod-product-compliance
Ingram Content Group UK Ltd.
Pitfield, Milton Keynes, MK11 3LW, UK
UKHW021907190726
13853UKWH00002B/546